· REVISED & UPDATED ·

SAM E. STONE

How to Be an
Effective Church Leader

FOREWORD BY DAVE STONE

How to Be an Effective Church Leader is also available on videocassette from
Good News Productions International, P. O. Box 222, Joplin, MO 64802.

Cover design by Mark A. Cole

Library of Congress Cataloging-in-Publication Data
Stone, Sam E.
    How to be an effective church leader / Sam E. Stone.— [Rev. ed.].
        p.   cm.
    Includes bibliographical references.
    ISBN 0-89900-899-2 (pbk.)
    1. Christian leadership. I. Title.
BV652.1 .S76 2001
253—dc21

                                                    2001047358

To my parents
who led me to love
and serve Jesus

FOREWORD

As a child, I remember playground arguments often settled with a childish shout, "It takes one to know one!" A youngster usually pulled out this phrase as a last resort when he had been called some unflattering label.

How to Be an Effective Church Leader is a positive reflection on the childhood comment, "It takes one to know one." This book, written by Sam Stone, (better known to me as "Dad") is the product of one who knows the church and one who knows what it takes to lead the church.

My father knows what it means to be an effective church leader because that's exactly what he has been for the past 40 years. His experience as an associate minister, preacher, editor of a Christian magazine (for over 20 years), and an elder in the local church, provides the reader with a great well from which to drink.

Some books on leadership don't really scratch where people itch. They simply expound and confuse. But the questions answered in this book are the ones that leaders are asking *today*. The material is practical, easy-to-read, and vital to anyone in ministry. The illustrations come right out of the life of the church, making it easy for you to draw parallels with your ministry.

If I tried to describe my dad in one word I would choose the word "balanced." His steady and faithful commitment to the truth of the Bible is unwavering, and yet his leadership is always tempered with grace.

This concept called "leadership" can be a tough one to figure out. *How to Be an Effective Church Leader* can help unravel the mystery for you. Leading the church involves knowing people. You can't lead people if you don't understand them. Each chapter will inspire you to lead in the same way that Sam Stone's life has inspired my brother and me to pursue being leaders in the church.

If you read this book and put the principles into practice, Dad would say that you *can* become an effective Christian leader. If anyone should know that, it would be Sam Stone. After all, it takes one to know one!

Dave Stone
Southeast Christian Church
Louisville, Kentucky

How to Be an Effective Church Leader

CONTENTS

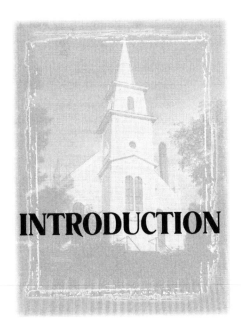

INTRODUCTION

The local church holds the key to the future of Christianity.

Your local church. Mine.

The college, the weekly church-sponsored TV program, the publishing house, and the mission may be desirable and valuable, but if New Testament Christianity is to succeed, it must flourish at the grassroots level.

No church will be stronger than its leaders. Its greatness begins with them. Every great movement in history started with great leaders. For the church to do its best work, effective leadership is essential.

> *No church will be stronger than its leaders.*

The inspired record of the New Testament shows us what the church was like when Jesus established it through the apostles. The church began on

Pentecost in Jerusalem after Christ's resurrection (Acts 2). It was composed of those believers who had repented of their sins and had been baptized (Acts 2:37-41).

In those early days, the apostles led the church (Acts 6:2). As their workload increased, they urged Christians to choose from among themselves some men who could be placed in charge of specific duties. These workers are referred to as "servants" or "deacons" (Acts 6:1-6). The first deacons were appointed to distribute food to the area widows.

When persecution came, the believers were scattered (Acts 8:4). The apostles made missionary journeys and established churches across a wide area. Wherever they established a church, they helped train and set apart groups of local leaders to direct the activity after they moved on. These local leaders were called elders (Acts 14:23; 15; 20:17ff) and sometimes pastors and bishops. All three titles are used interchangeably in Scripture.

Paul gave special directions to these men in his letters to his assistants Timothy and Titus. His advice for first-century church leaders still applies today. The principles given in God's Word can help those who lead the local church.

A good leader is one who knows the way, goes the way, and shows the way.

A congregation will not be greater than its leaders. If we have untrained, uncommitted, and uninformed people directing the local church, the future is bleak. But if we have those who are dedicated, educated, and motivated, we can be optimistic.

This book offers practical ideas for all who are now or hope to be servant leaders in the church.

A good leader is one who knows the way, goes the way, and shows the way. If you want to be such a leader, read on!

WHO RUNS THE CHURCH?

In this chapter:
✔ Jesus' right to leadership
✔ Jesus' leadership role
✔ Jesus' requirements for church leaders

Journalist Brock Brower wrote that if Martian spacemen were to descend to our planet and demand, "Take me to your leader," the earthlings would not know where to direct them. This problem exists in the church as well.

Who runs the church? For those who trust the Bible to be their sole authority, the answer should be easy to find. Jesus Christ is the head of the church. This fact underlies everything else said in this book. Paul tells us, "God placed all things under his feet and appointed him to be head over everything for the church, which is his body, the fullness of him who fills everything in every way" (Ephesians 1:22,23).

Most Christians, if questioned on the subject, would agree that Jesus is the head of the church. You won't find many people in the church willing to bow down to an idol or swear allegiance to some human authority. Yet in practice some deny that Jesus is the head of the church even while they affirm it in words. They deny it when they follow the direction of some school, publishing house, or denominational organization instead of the Word of God. Jesus Christ is the only true authority for the church.

The church is not a democracy.

People deny the authority of Christ in another way when they treat the church as a democracy, believing that its authority rests in a majority vote either of the congregation or some governing board.

The church is not a democracy. It is ruled by Jesus Christ. Seth Wilson, longtime Dean of Ozark Christian College, has frequently talked to men's groups about the work of elders. He tells them:

> We do not own the church. We do not govern it. Christ bought it with His blood, and He is absolute head over everything pertaining to the church.
>
> No majority can ever be large enough to set aside His will on anything, or to establish any other rule over His people. Every so-called vote by any member or officer of the church must not express our right to decide or to rule. It must express the consent each of us gives to a person or a policy as being what Christ wants for His church.
>
> We do not have a right to vote in the church as in a democracy, but we have a duty to God to express our understanding of His will for us and to work for agreement with others concerning His will. A vote may not settle what is the Lord's will; it may only begin a devoted study and effort to clarify it for all the members. If Christ's will can be found in the Bible, we should find it, clarify it, and accept it without voting. ("The New Testament Picture of Elders of the Church," *Christian Standard*, October 22, 1978, p. 4.)

All who lead in the church must first be followers. We must follow our one Lord, obedient to His will. Any exercise of authority on our part stands under His judgment.

HIS RIGHT

Jesus has every right to be head of the church. It is His right first because of creation. "By him all things were created. . . . And he is the head of the body, the church" (Colossians 1:16-18). God made us. We belong to Him. What right do we have to be proud of our looks, our talents, our abilities? They are His—He gave them to us. Perhaps we should say He lent them to us. Who are we to question His will?

Christ also has the right to be head of the church because of redemption. The poignant love story of the Old Testament prophet Hosea preaches a sermon every time we hear it. He was willing to buy back his own bride, making her twice his. So did Jesus. He not only created us but He redeemed us from sin as well. In the words of the old hymn,

> The Church's one foundation
> Is Jesus Christ her Lord;
> She is His new creation
> By water and the word:
> From Heav'n He came and sought her
> To be His holy bride;
> With His own blood He bought her,
> And for her life He died.

("The Church's One Foundation" by Samuel J. Stone.)

HIS ROLE

The term "head" can suggest different things. We may think of a general and his army, a king and his subjects, or a shepherd and his sheep. Paul uses the term, however, to mean the head of a human body in relation to its various other parts. Thinking of it that way, what does your head do?

The head expresses the body's feelings. When you touch a hot stove, the nerve endings in your fingers send a message to the head. The head, in turn, sends a message to the mouth. The mouth opens and you yell, "Ouch!" Of course it happens a little faster than you can read about it! The head expresses the body's feelings.

What is true for the human body has a far more beautiful parallel in Scripture. Paul explains, "In the same way, the Spirit helps us in our weakness. We do not know what we ought to pray for, but the Spirit himself intercedes for us with groans that words cannot express. And he who searches our hearts knows the mind of the Spirit, because the Spirit intercedes for the saints in accordance with God's will" (Romans 8:26,27).

> *What is true for the human body has a far more beautiful parallel in Scripture.*

The head is aware of the body's needs. Right now it may be saying, "You should have had more sleep last night! Quit staying up to watch so much television!" Your head knows when you are hungry, thirsty, cold, hot, afraid, or whatever. The head knows all about the body.

That's the way it is with Christ and the church. He knows what Christians need. He knows we need love, worship, study, and fellowship—and He provides these things through the local church.

The head determines the body's response. At least it does as far as it can. I used to play basketball regularly thirty years ago, but I don't do it much now. I still know what I should do when I'm under the basket fighting for a rebound. My head says, "Jump!" but my body says, "Who, me?"

Since Jesus provides for His people by means of the local church, it follows that we Christians are not only the recipients of His care but also the agents of it. Those of us who serve as leaders in Christ's church need to be sensitive to the needs of others, responding to them in love as we are motivated and directed by our head.

The head tells us what to do and, if we can do it, we act as directed. So it is with Christ. He has all authority in the church.

HIS REQUIREMENTS

Christ rules the church. Leaders in any local congregation are servants under His authority. For each of us, three things are required.

We must know His Word. If Christ is head of the church, and if we are a part of His body, we should know what He says in His revealed Word, the Bible.

Too many of us are like the fellow who applied for a job. His prospective employer said, "For a person with no experience, you're certainly asking for a high wage."

The man replied, "Well, the work's a lot harder when you don't know what you're doing."

That's true! We ought to know what God has said. Every leader needs to spend time in Bible study and Scripture memorization. Paul wrote, "Let the word of Christ dwell in you richly as you teach and admonish one another with all wisdom" (Colossians 3:16). Men's opinions and official pronouncements will come and go. Only God's Word abides.

We must wear His name. Those committed to Christ should proudly wear their Master's name. The name "Christian" is biblical (Acts 11:26; 26:28; 1 Peter 4:16). It frees one from allegiance to any denomination or human authority. One day all people will confess that Jesus is Lord (Philippians 2:11). The believer may be ridiculed or persecuted for such a statement, but on the last day, Jesus will be shown to be our only hope for salvation.

We must obey His will. Saying we are "Christians" means more than talking about it. We must show we are His. God plainly declared, "This is my Son, whom I love. . . . Listen to him!" (Matthew 17:5). When Jesus affirmed His complete authority over the church (Matthew 28:18-20), He directed His followers to evangelize the world and edify each convert. Doing what Jesus said is the church's task.

Lyman Beecher was one of the most famous preachers of the nineteenth century. Someone asked him how he was able to accomplish so much in his church. He replied, "Oh, I preach on Sundays and four hundred of my members preach every day." That will do it! This is why Boston noticed the church where Beecher ministered. Any church in any place can grow when members honor the church's head.

Henry David Thoreau wrote, "If a man does not keep pace with his companions, perhaps it is because he hears a different drummer. Let him step to the music which he hears." Do you hear God's call? Are you living within His will? Will you march to the sound of His drum?

Becoming More Effective

Through Action:

Study each Scripture reference cited in this chapter in its context. Note any new insights concerning Christ's role and man's role in the church.

Through Reading:

Beausay, William II. *The Leadership Genius of Jesus: Ancient Wisdom for Modern Business.* Nashville: Thomas Nelson, 1997.

Briner, Bob. *The Management Methods of Jesus: Ancient Wisdom for Modern Business.* Nashville: Thomas Nelson, 1996.

Briner, Bob, and Ray Pritchard. *The Leadership Lessons of Jesus: A Timeless Model for Today's Leaders.* Nashville: Broadman & Holman, 1997.

Lawson, LeRoy. *The New Testament Church Then and Now.* Cincinnati: Standard Publishing, 1996, revised.

Questions to Ponder

(These questions have been provided for each chapter by the Publisher)

1. In what specific ways are churches today failing to respect the complete authority of Christ?

2. Do you know of any church (or denomination) that does not trust the Bible to be their sole authority for faith and practice?

3. Why do you think various churches have stopped trusting the Bible to be their sole authority?

4. Give an example of someone you know who followed the direction of some school, publishing house, or denominational organization instead of the Word of God.

5. How can we be better followers—more obedient to our head, Jesus Christ?

6. What hurdles/stumbling blocks are keeping you from honoring your head?

Looking Ahead:

What makes a good leader? Before reading the next chapter, ponder what qualities you consider essential for an effective church leader to possess.

2

WHAT MAKES A GOOD LEADER?

In this chapter:
✔ Choose leaders who are willing to do the job
✔ Be sure the candidate's faith is solid
✔ Allow his ability to be demonstrated in small ways first
✔ Look at his lifestyle

Church leaders wear different titles. For each job the qualifications may differ, but for most leadership positions, the basic requirements are similar.

The qualifications for elders and deacons can be found in 1 Timothy 3. These inspired instructions of the apostle Paul offer practical insights for all generations in all parts of the world.

You and I may differ on what makes a good leader. A person's worth or ability depends on who is doing the evaluating, and we may not always see eye to eye on all points of comparison. The important thing is to consider the basic guidelines laid down in Scripture for all leaders. In 1 Timothy 3, four principles stand out.

WILLINGNESS

"If anyone sets his heart on being an overseer, he desires a noble task," Paul begins (3:1). The potential elder (bishop, overseer, pastor) must demonstrate a desire to serve.

An office in the church is not an honor to be granted, nor an award for attendance or giving. Certainly it is not a way to try to get a slacker to become active! Instead it is a serious God-given place in the kingdom. No one should be placed in office if he has to be "talked into it." He should have sufficient love for the Master and sufficient respect for the confidence of the church that he would desire to help in any way possible.

In New Testament times, this willingness to serve meant sacrifice. Those selected were being asked to work (Acts 6:1-3), not just to fill a position.

No one should be placed in office if he has to be "talked into it."

Many churches today wisely offer a full explanation of their expectations to one who is chosen to lead. They have drawn up job descriptions for such positions as Christian education director, youth sponsor, or committee chairperson. Before one is placed in a position of leadership, he or she needs to know what is expected.

If one's family is not sympathetic, he may find that it is not enough to have the desire to work. This is why many churches invite the person's spouse to training classes as a way of underscoring the job expectations.

Because one is willing to serve, it does not follow that he must think of himself as the perfect deacon or VBS director, ideally qualified for the position. Humility is essential. All Christians ought to live in a way that prepares them for church leadership.

FAITH

In Ephesus it was critical that elders and deacons be men whose lives were built on bedrock faith. Such faith is still critical today. Attacks on biblical Christianity continue to the present. The labels and leaders may vary, but deviation from the truth is still the norm for many. Leaders today must be able to say with Paul, "I am not ashamed of the gospel, because it is the power of God for the salvation of everyone who believes" (Romans 1:16).

A church must be cautious not to place in office a man who is not fully committed to the teachings of the New Testament. The qualifications for an elder obviously make deep faith essential, but notice that the requirement of faith is also specified for deacons. Commenting on 1 Timothy 3:9, Bible scholar Donald Guthrie observed that "the deacons are to be men not merely of practical acumen, but also of spiritual conviction."[1] The evidence of such strong faith was the faith and behavior of the leader's children (Titus 1:6).

Paul was equally concerned to secure leaders who would hold firmly to the faith, as he emphasized in his letter to Titus. The brethren in Crete had been taught a trustworthy message; now they must stay with it. The leader must also be able to "encourage others by sound doctrine and refute those who oppose it" (v. 9).

Some get the wrong idea. They think faith is believing something you know isn't so. Not at all. Trust is based on evidence. When you see what God has done in the past, you have confidence in what He will do in the future. "Now faith is being sure of what we hope for and certain of what we do not see" (Hebrews 11:1).

Abraham believed God. He put his life in the Lord's hand. Whatever God said, Abraham would do. That is faith. Like all of us, Abraham could not honor God by doing His will perfectly. But he could honor God by being fully persuaded that God would keep His word, even though it might seem to involve an impossibility. We can have that kind of faith, too.

Noah's faith rested on God. No weather forecast predicted rain. No scientific evidence would have led him to build an ark in a desert land. Here was faith. Noah's trust in God caused him to act in obedience to the divine command. Faith always does. If a man says he believes in the Lord while refusing to obey Him, it shows that he lacks biblical faith.

Amid the pressures of modern society, remember Moses. "He considered the 'reproach of Christ' more precious than all the wealth of Egypt, for he looked steadily at the ultimate, not the immediate reward" (Hebrews 11:26, J. B. Phillips). This is what faith does. It takes us beyond the desire to do whatever seems to work best for the moment—surely an underlying fault of our day.

Men are ready to lie if it will get them out of trouble, to cheat if it will help them pass a test, to misrepresent facts if it will make them a few more dollars, to be immoral if it will give them pleasure. But this is not God's way. It is the way of doubt and disbelief.

The great galaxy of the saints in the roll call of the faithful (Hebrews 11:32-38) were willing to die for what they believed. They trusted God. They were willing to risk everything for Him. Church leaders (and followers, too) must have the same confident, expectant trust that marked the faithful people of Scripture.

We need leaders of faith today like Robert Morrison, who set sail as a missionary for China amid considerable ridicule. Someone asked Morrison if he thought that he—one man—could make much of an impression on such a great nation as China, so long embedded in another religion. He replied, "I can do very little, if anything. However, I expect God will." And God did.

He will with our lives, too, if we commit them unreservedly to Him in faith.

ABILITY

Both elders and deacons are required to demonstrate their ability before they are placed in a position to serve. The requirements are similar for the two offices, but for the elder, greater emphasis is placed on ability. The elder must also be "able to teach" (1 Timothy 3:2). Both elder and deacon must be able to manage their children and their own households well. "If anyone does not know how to manage his own family, how can he take care of God's church?" (v. 5).

If a man can discipline his own children graciously and wisely, he may be entrusted with a larger responsibility. This fits with the principle shown in the parable of the talents (Matthew 25:14-30). Potential skill in a larger sphere can be indicated by similar skill in a lesser sphere.

An individual should prove himself as an active member of a local congregation for a time before he is considered as a candidate for office. I feel this principle holds true even when a longtime Christian moves from one community to another. For example, when our family moved from Clovis to Albuquerque, New Mexico, we placed our membership with a church in our new home city. Back in Clovis my father had been an elder, the chairman of the board, and the teacher of a men's class. Was he immediately placed into those positions in the new church? No. Should he have been? No. But in the years that followed, my dad was made an elder, then chairman of the board, and also a Sunday-school teacher.

An elder is responsible to pastor the flock. Yet a new shepherd does not even know the sheep, and the sheep certainly do not know his voice. A potential elder, no matter how well qualified in other ways, needs time to get to know the members of the congregation he will help lead.

Each congregation must determine the ability of a person for itself and accept the responsibility of placing qualified candidates in office. Those with the ability who also meet the other qualifications will not find themselves without the opportunity to serve.

LIFE

A church leader must receive favorable testimony from two groups— those within the church and those outside it (1 Timothy 3:7). One may appear very religious to those who see him only on Sunday mornings. To his coworkers on the job, he may look quite different!

The various qualifications listed in 1 Timothy 3 speak of a man's way of life: "temperate, self-controlled, respectable, hospitable . . . not given to drunkenness, not violent but gentle, not quarrelsome, not a lover of money" (vv. 2-3). Testing in life must precede appointment to positions of service and leadership (vv. 6,10).

Someone put the matter into verse:

> You write a sermon a chapter a day
> > By the deeds that you do and the words that you say;
> Men read what you write, whether false or true,
> > So what is the gospel according to you?

Robert Moffatt, missionary to savage tribes of South Africa, translated the Bible into the native language and taught the people to read. He watched the remarkable changes which the gospel brought in the lives of these formerly fierce warriors. He saw them show mercy and compassion to enemies and to the weak and helpless.

One day a native with a dog on a leash came running up. "My best hunting dog is ruined—and it's your fault," the native said.

Moffatt examined him "I see nothing wrong."

"But I know he is ruined. He ate some pages from the Bible you gave me."

Moffatt laughed. "That won't hurt."

"But it will," argued the native. "I have seen the Bible in the heart of a man change him from a fierce warrior to a meek, peaceful neighbor. If it will do that to a man, I know that my dog will never again be fierce enough to be a good hunting dog."

We may smile at this man's misunderstanding of how God's Word operates—but he had learned one vital truth: the gospel does work! It does change lives.

The person who is chosen to lead the Lord's church must demonstrate behavior changed by the power of the gospel.

The person who is chosen to lead the Lord's church must demonstrate behavior changed by the power of the gospel.

As we evaluate those who serve as leaders in the local church, these biblical qualifications must be kept paramount.

1. Donald Guthrie, *The Pastoral Espistles* (Grand Rapids: Eerdmans, 1986), p. 84.

Becoming More Effective

Through Action:

Prepare a job description based on Scripture for one or more of these positions: elder (pastor), deacon, minister (evangelist).

Through Reading:

Guiness, Os, ed. *Character Counts: Leadership Qualities in Washington, Wilberforce, Lincoln, & Solzhenitsyn.* Grand Rapids: Baker, 2000.

Maxwell, John C. *The 21 Indispensible Qualities of a Leader.* Nashville: Thomas Nelson, 1999.

Olasky, Marvin. *The American Leadership Tradition: The Inevitable Impact of a Leader's Faith on a Nation's Destiny.* Wheaton, IL: Crossway, 2000.

Strauch, Alexander. *Biblical Eldership: An Urgent Call to Restore Biblical Church Leadership.* Revised and Expanded. Littleton, CO: Lewis-Roth, 1995. (Available through College Press.)

Questions to Ponder

1. Who should screen candidates for church leadership positions? How may this best be done?

2. What is your belief concerning the author's statement "No one should be placed in office if he has to be 'talked into it'"?

3. Does your church have clearly articulated expectations for its leaders? Is the entire congregation aware of these expectations?

4. The author states that every Christian ought to live in such a way as to prepare himself for church leadership. Do you agree?

5. What would be some ways to prepare for future leadership opportunities?

6. The author discussed four categories (willingness, faith, ability, and life) of the qualities necessary to be a church leader. Do you think that any one of these is any more important than the others? Why or why not?

Looking Ahead:

There are many things that might occupy the thoughts, time, and energy of a church leader. What do you think should be the top priority of every leader in the Lord's church? Our next chapter addresses this question.

3

WHAT'S MOST IMPORTANT?

In this chapter:
✔ Be a student of the Word
✔ Talk to God on a regular basis
✔ Search out other tools to help you grow (books, music, life experiences, etc.)

God is concerned with *what we are*, not just *what we do*. Some Christian leaders seem oblivious to the implications of the message they profess. They teach about Christian behavior, attend seminars on fighting moral evil in the community, or dis-

> *God is concerned with what we are, not just what we do.*

cuss the need for devotion, but at the same time they fail to realize that the message must first be lived out in their own lives.

Such undiscerning individuals remind one of the Boston minister who saw some urchins clustered about a dog of doubtful pedigree. "Well, what are you fellows up to?" he asked.

"Swapping lies," said one. "Whoever tells the biggest one gets the pup."

"Boys! I'm shocked!" The preacher replied. "When I was your age I never thought of telling an untruth!"

"You win!" the kids chorused. "The dog's yours!"

We all have our inconsistencies. It's not enough to *look like* a Christian leader. What's really important?

Your relationship with God.

Leaders, of all people, must recognize this. Paul did. He compared himself to an athlete in training for a race or a fight. He explained, "I beat my body and make it my slave so that after I have preached to others, I myself will not be disqualified for the prize" (1 Corinthians 9:27).

Paul told a young church leader in the first century, "Train yourself to be godly. For physical training is of some value, but godliness has value for all things, holding promise for both the present life and the life to come" (1 Timothy 4:7,8).

Training is as important for the Christian leader as for the athlete. When he was just a boy, Tiger Woods was started on the path to winning golf championships by his father. He tells young people today how he learned discipline at an early age. He still practices regularly. Top athletes pay the price of regimented training.

Keeping up one's relationship with God is not easy for anyone, but for a Christian leader it becomes harder yet. The leader is expected by others to be "spiritual." He may begin acting more religious than he is. He wants to keep up appearances. This was the problem of the Pharisees.

It can be hard to find time for daily devotions or even attendance at church study/service functions. The busier you become in "church business," the less time you have available for your own personal spiritual development.

Worship can present another problem. Church leaders are frequently doing something in the services. They are not able just to sit, concentrate on the service, and enjoy heartfelt worship. One leader may be thinking of what he is supposed to do next; another trying to remember a meeting coming later; musicians and ushers are concentrating on their assignments; elders and deacons may have their minds on Communion and the offering. Yet worship requires one's conscious effort. What are some of the ways church leaders can work to grow spiritually?

READ THE BIBLE REGULARLY

Whatever your responsibilities, you need to budget time for personal, devotional reading of God's Word. It is easy to excuse negligence in Bible reading by saying, "I'm really involved with the Bible all the time. I get lessons for my class. I'm in the worship service. I hear a lot about the Bible." But such secondhand Bible study cannot replace your own reading and study.

Even a minister is tempted to read the Bible only for sermons, lessons, addresses, and articles. He reads it to find something to say to someone else. This is not enough. He first must read it to see what God is saying to him.

The psalmist declared, "Thy word have I hid in mine heart, that I might not sin against thee" (Psalm 119:11, KJV). Today many seem content to stop with the first five words: "Thy word have I hid"!

Our Bible lies on the table underneath the newspaper or sports magazine. Like medicine, it doesn't help unless we use it. But when we do, God's Word heals our spiritual ills. Whatever method or schedule of Bible reading we intend to use, we must decide to reserve a specific time in our daily schedules to read from the Word of God. Many varied plans of Bible reading have been suggested:

1) Reading nine chapters a day takes one through the New Testament every month. This could be done in about thirty minutes each day.

2) Four or five chapters a day will take one through the entire Bible in a year.

3) Variations include dividing the Bible into sections and reading one book from each section consecutively. Other plans provide ideas for reading some from the Old Testament and some from the New Testament each day.

4) Follow a Bible reading plan such as a "Bible Book of the Month" like *Discipleship Journal's* Bible reading plan, which can be found online at **www.navpress.com/dj-brp.asp** or the Bible reading plan published in the last issue each year of *The Lookout* magazine.

5) A Chinese man who became a Christian had as his motto, "No Bible, no breakfast." He would never eat in the morning until he first had read his Bible.

6) Billy Graham has stated that he attempts to read five Psalms and one chapter of Proverbs every day. He says, "I read Psalms to keep right with God and Proverbs to keep right with man." This takes you through both books every month.

SPEND TIME IN PRAYER

"Make your spare moments prayer moments," someone has said. It is even better to plan regular times of prayer. Such times may differ for each person, but they must be planned.

One Christian leader said, "By the grace of God and the strength of His Holy Spirit I desire to lay down the rule not to speak to man until I have spoken to God."

"Make your spare moments prayer moments."

For me, driving to work provides a good time to pray. After listening to the latest news, weather, and traffic report, I turn off the car radio and spend time in prayer. I start out by singing a Christian hymn or chorus, which helps focus my mind on God. Then I can unburden my heart to the Lord as I drive. This is one time when it is best not to close your eyes and bow your head!

Certainly we will pray at mealtimes and before classes, board meetings, and committee meetings. We may choose to use some tools to help us, such as a prayer list. Teachers and youth sponsors may pray daily for their students. Elders may pray for those in their "flocks." Every leader can remember those having needs who are listed in the church newsletter or bulletin. We may want also to consider another helpful spiritual discipline—praying the prayers found in Scripture.

"Pray without ceasing" is the biblical command that calls for a spirit of prayer in all of life (1 Thessalonians 5:16). We need constant communication with God throughout the day. When you want to control your temper, when you need to resist temptation, when you want to say the right word to help another, when you prepare to serve—pray.

FIND OTHER WAYS TO GROW

While the Bible should have first priority in our reading, other excellent resources are also available. Books and periodicals from Christian publishers provide helpful tools for spiritual growth. In addition to Bible studies and how-to books, you may find biographies of Christian leaders to be a constant encouragement.

Some Christian television programs and videocassettes can be helpful. Here, as in all reading and viewing, discrimination is essential. However popular the writer, speaker, or singer may be, his or her message must be tested by its fidelity to God's unchanging Word.

Christian music can be inspiring, too. Radio programs, tapes, and CDs can all help fill your mind with helpful thoughts as you travel. There are other ways to use the time spent driving for spiritual development. One might listen to cassette tapes of Scripture or tapes from conferences. Or you might write out a Bible verse or outline you wish to memorize and place it on the visor or dashboard. By glancing at it as you go, you can make driving time do double duty.

Plan times for spiritual renewal. Every leader needs such times. A busy person may be tempted to think such times are wasteful and could be better spent serving his congregation in some way. But the time isn't wasted. As pioneer evangelist Charles Reign Scoville said, "The time isn't lost in lifting a pile driver, and the time isn't lost when a Christian stops to pray."

The familiar words of Ecclesiastes remind us that "for everything there is a season." Many things are essential for a full, useful life. You need not attend church for eight hours a day—but, on the other hand, do you need to spend a couple of hours each day watching TV, reading the newspaper, or surfing the Internet? The important thing is never to be employed by trifles. The priorities in your life should be ordered; each in its proper place. "Seek ye first the kingdom of God, and his righteousness" (Matthew 6:33, KJV).

That's what is most important!

Becoming More Effective

Through Action:

Secure information about cassette tapes that can be used for leadership development. Many church leaders have expressed appreciation for the Injoy series of audiocassette training materials offered by John Maxwell (Web site: **www.injoy.com**). His seminar on "Developing Leaders to Make a Difference" suggests ways to develop a new generation of leaders. Maxwell's four-part video series *Develop the Leader within You* (Thomas Nelson, publisher) also provides practical help.

Through Reading:

Ortberg, John. *The Life You've Always Wanted: Spiritual Disciplines for Ordinary People.* Grand Rapids: Zondervan, 1996.

Peterson, Eugene. *A Long Obedience in the Same Direction: 20th Anniversary Edition.* Downer's Grove, IL: InterVarsity, 2000.

Sanders, J. Oswald. *Spiritual Leadership.* Rev. ed. Chicago: Moody, 1999.

Willard, Dallas. *The Divine Conspiracy: Rediscovering Our Hidden Life in God.* San Francisco: HarperCollins, 1998.

Questions to Ponder

1. Do you agree or disagree with the author's assessment that the personal relationship the church leader has with the Lord is of the utmost importance? Why or why not?

2. Could you relate to the distractions a leader has during the worship service? What could be done to limit, if not eliminate, these distractions?

3. Not every Bible reading plan is for everyone. Which of the suggestions by the author are you going to begin implementing immediately (if you don't already practice a specific plan)?

4. What have been the most inspiring lessons on prayer that you've been impacted by in recent years? How can you "follow through" with this important discipline in the upcoming days and weeks?

5. If someone were to ask you, "What resources should I devote my time and energy to in order to grow as a leader?" how would you reply?

Looking Ahead:

Have you ever looked into one of those special mirrors at amusement parks? You know, the ones that make you appear either very skinny or very overweight? Both reflections are false—because you know the true perception of yourself. Perception is vital to our understanding of church leadership. What do you perceive to be the key qualities that should be evident in the life of the church leader? The next chapter will elaborate on this theme.

4

WHAT'S EXPECTED OF ME?

In this chapter:
✔ Develop the mind of Christ
✔ Desire to be completely committed to the task
✔ See your position as an opportunity for service
✔ Remember the eternal rewards of a job well done

When you are selected to serve in some leadership capacity in the church, it is important to start out with the right perspective. How you view yourself and your task will affect your success. Three biblical principles need to be emphasized.

ATTITUDE AS WELL AS ACTION

"As [a man] thinks in his heart, so is he," we read in Proverbs 23:7 (NKJV). Freud said, "Thought is action in rehearsal."

Many of the Jews in Jesus' day had the idea that one's thoughts and motives didn't matter as long as a person did and said the right things. Our Lord removed that misconception. "The things that come out of the mouth come from the heart, and these make a man 'unclean'" (Matthew 15:18). "Guard your heart, for it is the wellspring of life" (Proverbs 4:23).

When you read the qualifications for a church officer in 1 Timothy 3 and elsewhere, you quickly find that the requirements include more than abilities and activities. God is interested in the person. Is he self-controlled, gentle, honest? When Peter described an elder, he emphasized the right attitude— willing, eager to serve, not domineering, being an example, clothed with humility (1 Peter 5:1-6).

Teamwork counts, whether on the football field or at a church board meeting.

Church leaders must have a healthy attitude because they are constantly involved in decision-making and in relations with people. No one can have his own way all the time; no one should expect to. A cooperative spirit, seeking the greatest good for the greatest number, is essential. Teamwork counts, whether on the football field or at a church board meeting. The Christian leader works diligently to bring about what is best for the church.

It always seems different for me than it is for the other guy. In a church paper years ago I found a witty illustration of that attitude.

When the other fellow takes a long time to do something, he's too slow; but when I take a long time to do something, I'm thorough.

When the other fellow doesn't do it, he's lazy; but when I don't do it, I'm too busy.

When the other fellow goes ahead and does something without being told, he's overstepping his bounds; but when I go ahead and do something without being told, that's initiative.

When the other fellow states his side of a question strongly, he's bullhead-ed; but when I state my side of a question strongly, I'm being firm.

When the other fellow overlooks a few of the rules of etiquette, he's rude; but when I skip a few rules, I'm original.

When the other fellow does something that pleases the boss, he's polishing the brass; but when I do something that pleases the boss, that's cooperation.

When the other fellow gets ahead, he sure had the lucky breaks; but when I manage to get ahead, man, hard work did that!

Funny, isn't it? Or is it?

Whenever individuals work together, friction is bound to occur. But if the oil of kindness and love is added to each situation, things can run smoothly. If you have the right uplook, you will have the right outlook. Harmony in interpersonal relationships is one way we may demonstrate the reality of Christ's presence in our lives. If each church leader has the right attitude, right actions will follow.

> *If each church leader has the right attitude, right actions will follow.*

CONSECRATION AS WELL AS ABILITY

In the closing section of 1 Timothy 5, the apostle tells both church members and leaders that they must live exemplary lives.

Avoid partiality. "Keep these instructions without partiality, and . . . do nothing out of favoritism" (v. 21). The Christian leader must be above prejudice. He must not show favoritism. He must not play politics.

Avoid impurity. Elsewhere the apostle commanded Timothy to flee youthful lusts. Here he emphasizes that the Christian leader must be a pure man. "Do not share in the sins of others. Keep yourself pure" (v. 22).

Those who like to seize upon verse 23 as justification for social drinking are faced with a problem. What Paul said was, "Stop drinking only water, and use a little wine because of your stomach and your frequent illnesses." Timothy had been trained in the Scripture. He had been taught the danger in strong drink. So scrupulous was he in his avoidance of it, that he wouldn't even take a medicine with alcoholic content (if we can put this in modern terms). Paul tells him to use a little wine for his illness. He encourages it for no other purpose.

Anticipate judgment. Some people do things so others can see. They're praised, thanked, honored, congratulated. Others have done some good deed that none have noticed. You may be in this category. You've worked quietly for the Lord doing some little job that most people don't even know about. You've never been thanked publicly, never been praised, and you feel taken for granted. Don't be disappointed. God knows—and God will repay.

Other people do wrong—they sin. They cause hard feelings. They injure others. They are wicked. And they seem to get by with it. Apparently they escape. Their sins seem to be so secretly committed, so cleverly disguised, that no one knows. They walk away, looking innocent. But God knows. And God will repay. "A man reaps what he sows."

Leaders in the church are called by God not only to be capable, but also to be dedicated to Him in their lives.

RESPONSIBILITY AS WELL AS HONOR

Beyond doubt, it is an honor to be selected as a church leader. Each member should hold the leadership in respect, honoring them for their good work. The late Guy P. Leavitt, longtime editor of *The Lookout*, often spoke to leaders. He would tell them:

> The church is the Lord's business. Its officers are the Lord's businessmen. Just as the church is the biggest and most important business on this earth, its leadership has the most important job in human experience. Every church officer worthy of his office wants to do his work better. He will have taken the first step in such improvement when he realizes that he was chosen, not primarily as an honor, but as employment to serve. His title is not honorary as much as it is an expression of confidence in him as one able to do good work. This opportunity to be of service should be uppermost in the mind of the church officer.

Sometimes we find those who want the honor, but not the responsibility. It takes time to be a church leader if you do the job right. Elders often have long meetings discussing the needs and problems in the church. Deacons may spend an entire day on a service project. Christian educators, music directors, and other leaders can all testify to the high time demands on those who serve in these specialized tasks.

The leader must have his priorities right. Christ and His church come first (Matthew 6:33). How can it be difficult for him to decide what to do on Sunday night? When the church is meeting, every leader should be present.

Faithful stewardship of time, talent, and treasure also goes with the job. Our church officers should set the example in sacrificial giving. No group of men in a congregation knows the financial needs better than they. They hear the treasurer's reports and try to disburse church funds wisely. A church will not reach above its leadership.

A church leader's spouse and family must share the commitment to Christ and His church. A wife can make or break her husband's work as an elder. If she enters into his ministry wholeheartedly, it will take on new life and power.

A church will not reach above its leadership.

In one congregation, an elder's wife became concerned that new members were not being assimilated into the church family. She began SNACK— Sunday Night After Church Koinonia. Once a month following the evening service she would invite new members along with some older members to their home. In an informal time of refreshments and fellowship these people were able to get better acquainted. Through this project, she greatly enhanced her husband's effectiveness and blessed the entire church.

When leaders take their responsibilities seriously, they find that they gain the respect and support of the membership. Every Christian has the duty to obey the command of Hebrews 13:7—"Remember your leaders, who spoke the word of God to you. Consider the outcome of their way of life and imitate their faith."

REWARD AS WELL AS SERVICE

When one begins to serve in leadership, he immediately finds new problems to solve, new crises to face, new difficulties to handle. It is easy to become discouraged. This is one reason Scripture teaches that no new convert should be placed in a position of leadership (1 Timothy 3:6,10).

But church leaders receive reward as well as service. We preachers have not always done as good a job as we should in pointing church leaders to that fact. All too frequently we list the qualifications and duties of an elder or deacon and stop there. We talk about what a church leader should be and do, then turn to other matters. But God promises reward for those who serve Him faithfully.

Of the deacon, Paul said, "Those who have served well gain an excellent standing and great assurance in their faith in Christ Jesus" (1 Timothy 3:13). Of the elder, he adds, "The elders who direct the affairs of the church well are worthy of double honor, especially those whose work is preaching and teaching" (1 Timothy 5:17).

Peter promises, "And when the Chief Shepherd appears, you will receive the crown of glory that will never fade away" (1 Peter 5:4).

True, much is required of a leader. True, people may criticize and misunderstand his best efforts. True, the demands may be great. But never forget, God rewards the faithful.

Never forget, God rewards the faithful.

Those who have served long and well in positions of leadership in the church can often tell of specific ways in which they have been blessed already. Many have found the truth of our Lord's promise, "Everyone who has left houses or brothers or sisters or father or mother or children or fields for my sake will receive a hundred times as much and will inherit eternal life" (Matthew 19:29).

One day the ultimate reward will be ours. Heaven awaits. Like Paul we can say, "I consider that our present sufferings are not worth comparing with the glory that will be revealed in us" (Romans 8:18). As the old song says, "There is joy in serving Jesus!"

Each Christian needs to say a word of encouragement to those who lead the local church. We must pray for them personally and as a group. They deserve our allegiance and obedience, for the sake of Christ. God's Word is plain. "Obey your leaders and submit to their authority. They keep watch over you as men who must give an account. Obey them so that their work will be a joy, not a burden, for that would be of no advantage to you" (Hebrews 13:17). Both leaders and followers must take care that they always follow Christ.

Becoming More Effective

Through Action:
Think of the church leader who has influenced you the most over the years. Try to write down what he did or said that helped you. What lessons can you learn from this?

Through Reading:
Maxwell, John C. *The Success Journey: The Process of Living Your Dreams.* Nashville: Thomas Nelson, 1997.

Maxwell, John C., and Jim Dornan. *Becoming a Person of Influence.* Nashville: Thomas Nelson, 1997.

Stone, Dave. *Keeping Your Head above Water: Refreshing Insights for Church Leaders.* Loveland, CO: Group, 2001.

Questions to Ponder

1. What are the specific duties and expectations for one in your present (or future) place of leadership?

2. How important is attitude to the overall effectiveness of the church leader? Why?

3. What steps do you think church leaders can take to ensure an improved attitude will result?

4. What are some precautionary measures church leaders can take today to help maintain purity?

5. The author states that "our church officers should set the example in sacrificial giving." Do you agree or disagree with his statement? Why or why not?

6. How well is your church doing at emphasizing the reward of serving as a church leader? What would be a way of doing this in your congregation?

Looking Ahead:

Have you ever been to a circus and seen the talented artist balancing a stack of fine china plates on each hand and his head? That's often the picture of the modern-day church leader—always balancing his many roles. How does one balance church work, family time, and one's marketplace responsibilities? We'll focus on this question in the next chapter.

5

HOW CAN I DO IT ALL?

In this chapter:
✔ Time management
✔ Priorities

The church leader has to do a balancing act. He runs the risk of giving too much attention in a single area. The wise leader will try to keep all of his responsibilities in perspective. His church work, important as it is, must not be allowed to assume an improper place in his life.

"How can you say that?" some gasp. "Isn't serving the Lord the only all-important thing?"

Certainly serving the Lord is important, but serving the Lord and serving the church are not synonymous. Some zealous workers think they must spend every waking hour doing "church work." They seem to think they are married to the church. The fact is, the church is already married! She belongs to Christ.

> *The fact is, the church is already married! She belongs to Christ.*

My first responsibility is to save my own soul. I ought to do "church work," but I have other duties commanded by God. I have a responsibility to my family, too. God expects me to take care of them.

This does not mean that you must throw up your hands in despair and never do anything in the local congregation until your children are grown. It does mean that you *must* manage your time well.

SCHEDULING

To start with, look at how you are spending your time now. Keeping a time log for a week is a revealing and humbling experience. Although we say we don't have time for some activities, the fact is that we all waste a great deal of time.

Next you must determine your priorities. Not everything is of equal importance. Your relationship to God comes first. Time for worship, study, and personal spiritual growth must have top priority. Then you must spend a certain amount of time at work to provide a living. You must spend time with your family. But that leaves a great deal of discretionary time. Out of this you can work for the Lord in various ways and you can rest, relax, and enjoy life.

The secret is in planning. Wise use of a calendar is a must. Mark down upcoming events well in advance. Just as you may turn in a vacation schedule at work six months or a year ahead, mark that (and other important dates) in your family planning calendar. Block out family days—times when you will be together, whether in or out of town. Record church activities. List annual events like retreats, conventions, revivals. Mark down regular meeting times for church officers, teachers, etc.

Then allot the time necessary for preparation for these activities. If you are in charge of the annual church picnic, for example, you may want to reserve the site six months to a year in advance. You might choose your committee several months ahead. As the time gets closer, you may even want to keep a half-day free to take care of last-minute details.

If you are asked to speak for a teacher appreciation banquet one month away, you may be tempted to look at the calendar, see that the night is free, and accept the invitation. What you should do is determine what subject you are to speak on and then decide how long it will take you to prepare that message properly. Preparation time must be included whenever you accept a responsibility.

Don't schedule your time too full. Time management experts suggest that one plan only 80 percent of his day. This allows a "cushion" to absorb unexpected, necessary interruptions. Contingency planning lets us respond to the real emergencies of life. Jesus taught that we must not be too busy to help those who need our help.

Preparation time must be included whenever you accept a responsibility.

You need free time, too. Allow time in the middle of any work period to relax, move around, and do something less demanding. Students are advised to have "bumper periods" during long hours of study.

There is no music in a rest, but there's the making of music in it. People are always missing that part of life's melody.

CHURCH ACTIVITIES

As we seek to balance our job, our church, and our home activities, we need to look for new ways of doing things, too. Creativity helps. All church meetings don't have to be held at night. A committee or board might have a breakfast meeting. You can meet with another church leader for lunch to outline plans. Try to combine activities.

A number of churches have avoided filling every weeknight with church activities. They found that they were wearing out their best workers. An hour-long Wednesday evening prayer/study program can be followed by various meetings. The first Wednesday might be for the elders; the second for the elders with the deacons; the third for committees (most individuals should not be serving on more than one); the fourth for Christian education (Sunday-school classes, youth sponsors, or VBS). Rather than taking two or more nights a week, a leader can come to the church on only one but attend two meetings.

Some congregations have found it helpful to serve supper on Wednesdays. This provides fellowship and allows working people to come to church without having to prepare a meal at home first.

The principle of combining activities holds true for individuals as well as congregations. Suppose you need to make some calls on church members. At the same time, you need to spend time with one of your children. Why not take your child with you? We found the value of this in our family. When my boys were still in grade school, I was serving as a preaching minister. I began taking one of the boys with me on the afternoons when I made calls.

The practice proved to be good in every way. We spent time together, talking between calls as we rode along. We might also run an errand or stop for ice cream afterwards. My boys soon felt more at ease meeting people and making new friends. They learned calling techniques, biblical truths, and some things about human nature at the same time. Both my sons are now in the ministry and they testify that this time spent calling was a positive experience.

FAMILY TIME

Whatever your task may be as a church leader, no job—secular or religious—is as important as your family. After God, your home must come first.

> *After God, your home must come first.*

"Providing" for your family means more than giving them food, clothes, and shelter. They need your time. As every older parent can tell you, children grow up and leave before you know it. If you don't spend time with them during their young, formative years, the chance to mold their lives is gone.

The Lord has used this aspect of life as a criterion for one who would be a church leader. Of the elder (overseer), Scripture declares, "He must manage his own family well and see that his children obey him with proper respect. (If anyone does not know how to manage his own family, how can he take care of God's church?)" (1 Timothy 3:4,5).

How can you do it all? You can't. No one can. Jesus couldn't, and neither can we. Best-selling writer and minister Charlie Shedd has observed:

> Our Heavenly Father never gives us too much to do. Men will. We assign ourselves an overload, but never the Lord. He knows what He wants from each of us, and there is plenty of time in His day for things essential to His plan. We do Him a grave injustice when we fall into the habit of compulsive overwork. We sin when we pressure out His wishes for assignments that have not been filtered through divine judgment.

We do God a grave injustice when we fall into the habit of compulsive overwork.

We need to pray with the psalmist, "Teach us to number our days aright, that we may gain a heart of wisdom" (Psalm 90:12).

Becoming More Effective

Through Action:

Keep a log of how you spend your time for one week. Note ways to improve your time usage, and work out a tentative schedule that can implement your plan.

Through Reading:

Asimakoupoulos, Greg, John Maxwell, and Steve McKinley. *The Time Crunch: What to Do When You Can't Do It All.* Portland: Multnomah, 1993.

Lewis, G. Douglass. *Meeting the Moment: Leadership and Well-Being in Ministry.* Nashville: Abingdon, 1997.

Smith, Ken. *It's about Time.* Wheaton, IL: Crossway, 1992.

Wright, Tim, and Lori Woods. *The Ministry Marathon: Caring for Yourself While You Care for the People of God.* Nashville: Abingdon, 1999.

Questions to Ponder

1. "The fact is, the church is already married! She belongs to Christ." What do you think of the church leader who gives more time, energy, and passion to church work than his own relationship with the Lord or with his family?

2. What are some of the things you do well to manage your time effectively? What are some scheduling areas that could be improved?

3. Why do you think we tend to feel guilty when we intentionally plan fun, play, rest time into our schedules? How important is this recreation time to our overall effectiveness as a church leader?

4. What could your church do to "combine activities" so as to not overload its leaders?

5. What are you doing to ensure you have quality "forming" time with your children? What steps can you take to ensure that they are being "molded" in the image of Christ?

6. How can you make sure you do not neglect your family?

Looking Ahead:

Running a marathon isn't easy. Neither is serving as a church leader. There will be plenty of high hills to climb and devilish plots to work through. How does the leader stay motivated in the midst of discouraging times? Let's learn together in the next chapter what we should focus on in order to keep pressing on.

WHAT KEEPS US GOING?

In this chapter:
✔ Develop a positive attitude
✔ Learn some psychology

A church nursery worker had her hands full with one little boy who was going through the "terrible twos." He often pushed the other children around. When his father came to pick up little Michael, he noticed him pulling a little girl's ponytail and making her cry. Scooping up his unruly offspring, he turned to the nursery director and said, "I would call Michael a bully, but since he's my son, I prefer to say he has 'leadership potential.'"

Unfortunately that is often the picture of a leader. But as the Scripture points out, it's not the right one. Jesus taught that a leader is not the boss, but

Jesus taught that a leader is not the boss, but the worker; not the lord, but the slave.

the worker; not the lord, but the slave. Every church leader knows what it is like to feel slighted and unrecognized. Most of us who deal with other people quickly find that some are hard to work with.

President Eisenhower once said, "Leadership is the art of getting somebody else to do something you want done because he wants to do it." This is known as motivation.

Church leaders must be motivated themselves and must know what keeps people going so they can encourage others to follow them.

YOUR ATTITUDE

An optimist has been defined as a person who, falling from the top of a forty-story building, says on the way down, "All right so far!" One does not have to overlook the facts to look on the bright side of life. Realism is necessary. But for the Christian, God must figure prominently in reality! The current situation is never as bad as it seems. A comedian once described status quo by saying, "That's Latin for the mess we's in!" The Christian leader will get in a mess occasionally. He will have problems. But he also has the assurance of God's Spirit to help him.

When you work in the church, you deal with people. They are Christian people, to be sure—but still people. They get discouraged, have their feelings hurt, and get upset just as other people do. Just as you do, in fact. By realizing your own inadequacies, you can be more sympathetic toward those of others. If you are not too proud to admit your mistakes, other people usually will be big enough to forgive you. They'll also be more willing to admit their mistakes.

When someone complains to you, what do you do? Don't fear the complaint. Don't ignore it. Don't deny it. A problem has to be solved. Assume that it can be solved. Work with the complainer, making it easy for him to modify his claims and cooperate. If you have done wrong, be willing to admit it. In this spirit, you can show the true humility that makes one willing to learn from others.

Paul said, "Follow my example, as I follow the example of Christ" (1 Corinthians 11:1). We cannot ask others to do just what we do—we must encourage them to do what the Lord asks. At the same time, we can't lead where we won't go ourselves. The Christian leader must seek to model the self-giving service taught by Christ and required of His followers.

The successful leader is one who knows others and knows what motivates them.

The successful leader is one who knows others and knows what motivates them. Management studies have listed these characteristics. Exceptional leaders

1) Have a high frustration tolerance.

2) Encourage participation by others.

3) Continually question themselves.

4) Are cleanly competitive.

5) Keep under control their "get even" impulses.

6) Win without exulting.

7) Lose without moping.

8) Recognize legal restrictions.

9) Are conscious of group loyalties.

10) Set realistic goals.

Such a leader is aware of life as it is and people as they are. He will plan, read, discuss, and arrange a strategy to accomplish his goals. Good leaders in the secular world follow this procedure regularly. In this as in other ways, the children of this world are sometimes wiser than the children of light.

UNDERSTANDING PEOPLE

To motivate someone, we must understand what makes him tick. One entire chapter in Kenneth Gangel's book, *Competent to Lead* (Moody Press, 1974), is devoted to a Christian analysis of motivation theory. Gangel points out that studies relating to employee/ employer relationships can be helpful for the church.

Man has an innate need to strive to become what he is capable of becoming.

Man has an innate need to strive to become what he is capable of becoming. In Maslow's "hierarchy of needs," we find ego needs (self-worth), social needs (belonging), security needs (protection from harm or from loss of employment), and finally physiological needs (food, activity, air, sleep).

Recognition of such needs helps a manager to make one's work more meaningful and fulfilling. On the other hand, to deny him such basic needs could hardly be a part of God's design.

In commenting on Maslow's approach, Gangel says:

> Once again an analysis of a secular theoretician in the light of the New Testament offers some striking insights. Surely we understand James to be saying that the communication of Christian theology to a man who is starving is sheer nonsense (James 2:14-20). His need for inner peace and eternal salvation is properly recognized by him only when physiological and safety needs have been met.
>
> On the other hand, a company (or a church) does not motivate a man by offering him additional fulfillment of needs that have already been met. When a man has enough bread, he is not impelled to action by the offer of more bread, or even by the potential wherewithal to buy more bread.
>
> What is there about Christian ministry that is self actualizing? Is it possible that the discouraged pastor or a Sunday school teacher ready to quit finds himself in that position because no one has taught him to think of his service as self-actualizing? Has the Christian-service dropout developed a distorted, slave-to-the-church concept of his task? Is it possible that the task itself has very little self-actualizing potential? (From *Competent to Lead*, by Kenneth

Gangel. Copyright 1974. Moody Press. Moody Bible Institute of Chicago. Used by permission.)

We attempt to treat others the right way, motivating them to do their best in advancing the cause of Christ. *The Royal Bank of Canada Monthly Letter* gave an excellent summary of what it means to motivate people:

> When you think about it, motivation is not much different from friendship. A friend attempts to understand you, and to help you as far as possible to achieve your aims. A friend is concerned about your happiness, and tries within the limits of his or her ability to make you happy. A friend is someone who supports you and knows that he or she can count on your support in return.
>
> Above all, a friend is someone who will go out of his or her way to do things for you. The motive for this is nothing more than the knowledge that you would do the same for him or her. And so it is with mutual motivation in the plant or office. The bosses who are most concerned about their subordinates get the most out of them in the form of high-quality work. (*The Royal Bank of Canada Monthly Letter*, 1980. Reprinted with the permission of the Royal Bank of Canada.)

TECHNIQUES

Approaching others to help in the work of the church always goes better when members can say, "This is what we are doing," not, "That's what they wanted." Each Christian needs to feel he is a vital part of an important task—not just a cog in the big machine operated by a few demanding leaders.

Suppose you need to secure more teachers, for example. As John Wilson, minister for many years with First Christian Church, Springfield, Ohio, pointed out, "Those who are invited to teach must understand that teaching the Word of God is a high privilege. They must be challenged with the importance of the task. The Bible school that has a reputation for solid Bible teaching because of the quality of teachers will attract committed workers. The key to recruiting is to help people find meaningful fulfillment in this avenue of service." Here are the steps outlined by Wilson:

1) Pray. God promises to hear us and lead us when we ask Him.

2) Enlist by personal invitation. Go to the person and tell him he is being considered as a teacher prospect. You cannot expect good results when a general appeal is made from the pulpit.

3) Explain in detail the need and appeal to the proper motive for responding. Don't downplay the task as something unimportant.

4) Promise to provide training and help in teaching.

5) Create favorable conditions for teaching. Work with teachers in solving problems that hinder and discourage good teaching.

6) Praise and encourage as the work deserves.

7) Keep the standards high.

8) Set a specified time for teaching. At the end of the time you can review the progress. Don't make it a "forever" task.

By staying in touch with workers and expressing appreciation to them, we can go a long way toward keeping them faithful and fruitful in ministry.

What keeps us going? After all is said and done, it is Jesus. We love Him and want to serve Him. With the proper support, guidance, and encouragement, we will. As we do, we can help others serve Him too.

Becoming More Effective

Through Action:

Use for a devotional time in your personal or group study *Leadership Meditations: Reflections for Leaders in All Walks of Life*, edited and selected by Dave Goetz (Wheaton, IL: Tyndale, 2001).

Through Reading:

DePree, Max. *Leadership Is an Art*. New York: Doubleday, 1989.

Gangel, Kenneth. *Feeding and Leading: A Practical Handbook on Administration in Churches and Christian Organizations*. Wheaton, IL: Victor, 1989.

Kouzes, James M., and Barry Z. Posner. *Encouraging the Heart: A Leader's Guide to Rewarding and Recognizing Others*. San Francisco: Jossey-Bass, 1999.

Shawchuck, Norman B., and Roger Heuser. *Leading the Congregation: Caring for Yourself While Serving the People.* Nashville: Abingdon, 1998.

Questions to Ponder

1. What helps keep you motivated on the job? What helps in your service for the Lord?

2. The leader has the assurance of God's Spirit to help him through the various problems that arise. How much of the Spirit's power do you think the average leader has tapped into? 100% ? 75%? 50%? 25%? 10%?

3. The leader must seek to model the self-giving service taught by Christ. What are some steps to take for the leader to ensure that this is a reality in his life and leadership?

4. Do you agree or disagree with the author's statement about the children of this world being wiser than the children of light? (See Luke 16:8.)

5. What can you and your church do to ensure that the spiritual *and* the "physiological and safety" needs are being met in the lives of the people you're trying to reach in your community?

6. Discuss how Jesus is our *best* source of motivation in ministry.

Looking Ahead:

One of the chief time commitments of the church leader is his attendance at the monthly board meeting (some churches may have board meetings more often). Do you look at these meetings with drudgery or delight? Our next chapter will help us enjoy participating in more efficient and inspirational meetings.

7

CAN I SKIP THE BORED MEETINGS?

In this chapter:
✔ The chairman should be a qualified administrator
✔ The meetings should be well organized
✔ Committees are the springboard to all-member involvement

A group of elders and deacons met in a Sunday-school classroom at the close of a long worship service. A stranger wandered in. "Could I help you?" one of them asked him.

"Well," said the stranger, "the preacher said there was to be a meeting of the bored in here—and I thought I should come."

Board meetings don't have to be bored meetings.

The work of the church is the most important business in the world. It deserves to be handled right. No meeting should be called just because the bylaws suggest it. If a meeting is not needed, skip it. In a well-organized and properly run church, leaders can have fewer meetings and shorter ones.

Board meetings don't have to be bored meetings.

At times the elders and deacons will need to meet together. At other times they may meet separately. If the elders are seen to be overseers of the total church program, they will set policies, lead in the ministry, and demonstrate loving concern for the flock.

Ideally the deacons will be putting their energies into active service projects. Many churches make one deacon responsible for an entire area of ministry, such as a bus ministry, benevolence, or building and grounds. He and those who work with him are given full charge of this sphere of service. They report regularly to the elders, bringing questions, problems, and suggestions to them as needed.

At the same time, the elders will want to keep the deacons informed of decisions and plans they have made. They will want their input on certain matters. Such joint meetings may fall under what has generally been known as a "board meeting." The principles that follow are applicable for any group meetings, however.

THE CHAIRMAN

The chairman is often the key to a good meeting. In consultation with the minister and church staff, he should prepare the agenda. A good chairman will not only handle meetings well, but will be effective in representing the board to the congregation. In some churches, it might also be his job to preside at congregational meetings.

Whether coming together as elders only, as elders and deacons, or as other church leaders, several things can be done to ensure meetings that are both pleasant and profitable.

One elder described the chairman's role like this: "The chairman should be one who enjoys his role and likes to work closely with people. He must possess ability to plan and delegate and must demonstrate his belief in the ability of a group to make decisions. He is responsible for employing techniques that will generate enthusiasm to the point where every member will make his best contribution."

THE PROCEDURE

Here are eight tips to make your meetings go more smoothly:

1) *Begin on time.* It is wise to set an ending time as well. If you begin on time and carefully observe your schedule, the members of your group will be more prompt as well.

2) *Follow an orderly plan.* The use of *Roberts Rules of Order* or similar guidelines need not make stiff, formal sessions. They can help you prevent problems and controversy. A relaxed, comfortable atmosphere is desirable. Some groups serve refreshments at each meeting. Sitting in a circle, in a semicircle or around a table can help, too. If the chairman keeps the group focused on the question before it, members will more easily move toward a decision.

3) *A printed agenda helps.* A printed agenda should be sent to every member of the group at least a few days before the meeting. With it can come any reports or recommendations that will need action. This will speed up the meeting and give members time to consider an issue before they are required to express an opinion on it.

4) *Attendance records are helpful.* At some churches, the board meetings include a roll call of members. Someone should at least keep tabs on the attendance of the group.

5) *Allow time for growth.* A devotional time should precede each meeting. Some church boards have a brief instructional period before conducting their business. Group members or staff teach on biblical or practical subjects.

6) *Make haste slowly.* Before presenting a new idea to the group, many church leaders discuss it first with others in the group or with the committee responsible for such a program. Do not ask for a decision on any important

matter until you know how it shall be put into effect. Decisions do not exist apart from their implementation.

7) *Use your committees.* Every possible item should be referred to a committee for investigation and a recommendation. This cuts down long discussions when all of the facts are not available. When a committee makes a report, the spokesperson can end with the words, "And we move that this be adopted and implemented." This brings the suggestion to the floor in a proper way.

8) *Keep a good spirit in the meetings.* Once in a while a particularly cantankerous individual may be placed on a board or committee with you. When this happened to me on one occasion, I read through the book of Proverbs, copying down the verses with relevant advice (Proverbs 3:30; 10:12; 15:1; 17:14). I wrote these on a small card and kept it on the table before me during each meeting. They helped! Many groups seek to avoid voting on matters and attempt to reach a consensus by which they will be governed. This, too, can be helpful.

> *Decisions do not exist apart from their implementation.*

COMMITTEES

In the modern church, good organization usually means good committees. Church work can be divided into general categories of work so that, as individual duties are handled, all may still be under the oversight of the elders.

Any size church can function under a committee system. The brand new congregation with twenty or thirty members will immediately become aware of matters that need attention. A committee system—perhaps with a deacon in charge of each service area—can expand as the church grows. Each committee should have a specific job. Temporary groups may be formed for special short-term needs.

Committees open the way for every-member ministry. Not only is it Scriptural to put each person to work, it is also beneficial because it works so well. If members are not involved, they will soon lose interest and may not remain faithful ("use them or lose them"). One job for each person and no more than one job for each person is a desirable goal.

Some excellent practical help on working with volunteers in various capacities in the local church is available. (Note the suggestions at the end of the chapter.)

Normally the minister is ex officio a member of all committees within the church. He is not to oversee or "boss" any committee, but to offer suggestions and comments. He can share in discussion like any other committee member.

Handling the business of the local church is not only practical and profitable, it is also Scriptural. The principle that Paul gave the church in Corinth many years ago still holds true: "Everything should be done in a fitting and orderly way" (1 Corinthians 14:40).

Becoming More Effective

Through Action:

Visit a growing, active church in your area to see how they carry out their program.

Through Reading:

Cionca, John. *Inviting Volunteers to Minister.* Cincinnati: Standard Publishing, 1999.

Stoesz, Edgar. *Meditations for Meetings.* Intercourse, PA: Good Books, 1999.

Treadwell, William, and Larry McSwain. *Church Organization Alive!* Nashville: Broadman, 1987.

Questions to Ponder

1. What factors do you think generally contribute to making meetings "bored" meetings?

2. How can we improve communication between various leaders and groups within our church?

3. What other qualities would you look for in the "chairman" of your church board in addition to the ones mentioned in this chapter?

4. As your church continues to grow, it will be imperative that committees be formed to meet the ever-increasing needs of the church family. Review the advice Moses' father-in-law Jethro gave in Exodus 18. How can you apply his advice to your present situation?

Looking Ahead:

There are many upfront, in-the-spotlight roles a leader must be involved in. Likewise, there are quite a few behind-the-scenes roles. Our next chapter will zoom in on several key leadership roles in the local church. Which do you feel is your temperament—upfront or behind-the-scenes leadership?

8

IS EVERYONE WATCHING ME?

In this chapter:
✔ Greeting people at the door allows one-on-one contact
✔ Begin up-front participation simply—with Scripture reading or prayer
✔ Be prepared to preside after growing your confidence in smaller ways
✔ Ushering offers a quiet path to up-front service

Some excellent potential leaders are reluctant to be named an elder or deacon because they are shy, quiet people. "I'm willing to serve, but I don't like to be up in front of people," they explain.

A church leader is viewed most when he is in the public eye. He prays at a morning worship service; he participates in a congregational meeting; he teaches a class. That is his job in the eyes of many. Actually these visible activities are only a small part of the church leader's work. Just as a football team requires many more players than the one who is carrying the ball, so the church must have more leaders than the one or two who happen to be seen by others.

It is true, however, that at times a church leader will be seen by others as he serves. The key to feeling at ease on those occasions is to remember why you are there. You are not in front of others to "make an impression" on them. You aren't seeking to draw attention to yourself. Your purpose is to serve God and help His people to do so.

> *Your purpose is to serve God and help His people to do so.*

Whenever I find myself getting nervous before I am to speak, I tell myself, "You are here to point others to Jesus." If you concentrate on getting your message across, you won't be worried about your appearance or what others may think of you. This principle holds true for any of the times we may feel on display.

GREETER

A good place for a shy person to begin serving is as a greeter. Standing inside the church door, you can speak a warm word of greeting to those coming for a service. All that is required is a smile, a handshake, and a friendly word.

If a stranger comes in, you can say, "Hi. I'm Bill Jones. I'm not sure that I have met you." If the person says, "I'm new in town," or "I've only been here once before," you can easily follow up with a nonthreatening question or two. You should concentrate on making the newcomer feel welcome.

If, on the other hand, the person says, "I've been a member here for twenty years," you can say, "Well, I'm glad to finally get to meet you. As our church grows, it's hard to keep up with everyone." You can then find out more about the person, repeating the name to help fix it in your mind for the future. Most people are sympathetic to the fact that no one can recall every other person's name at church!

Gradually a greeter gets acquainted (at least by face) with most of the people. This type of public service does not force you to speak to more than one or two people at a time. It also helps you feel comfortable with this group of people, since you will know most of them in a short while.

WORSHIP SERVICE PARTICIPANT

Taking part in the worship service can be started gradually. One way is to read the Scripture. In many congregations, a passage from the Bible is read at several points in the service—as a call to worship, before communion or a baptism, or in preparation for the sermon.

Effective Scripture reading requires preparation. Read the passage to yourself several times, being sure of the pronunciation and meaning of the words. Choose a copy of the Bible that has readable type. Mark the page and the place on the page. As you read it aloud (both before the service and when it is going on), take your time. Concentrate on getting across God's message, not worrying about how you sound or look.

Prayer is another good way to participate. If one is in the habit of talking to God regularly—and any church leader should be—it will not be difficult to offer a public prayer.

Some have been misled into thinking that public prayer means a loud and lengthy oration. That is not so. Jesus condemned the Pharisees for prayers like that. Most of our Lord's prayers were simple, brief, and to the point. Ours should be too.

Most of our Lord's prayers were simple, brief, and to the point. Ours should be too.

If you know ahead of time that you will be expected to lead in prayer, you can think of what you want to say and write it down if you prefer. It is no more wrong for a church leader to write out a prayer than for a minister to write out a sermon. As long as you mean what you say, your prayer can be pleasing to God.

PRESIDER

After you have participated in the services for a time, you will feel more comfortable about presiding at a meeting. The successful worship leader or presider needs to follow several guidelines.

1) Plan the service, or talk to those who are doing so, well in advance.
2) Write out the order, making any notes necessary to remind yourself of what to do when (for example, "Have congregation stand").
3) Arrive early.
4) Check to be sure that the microphone is on and that the lights, heat, etc. are properly adjusted.
5) Be sure each participant is present and knows what to do and when to do it.
6) Start on time.
7) Keep announcements to a minimum. Rather than standing up to introduce each separate part of the service, cover two or three items at a time, when possible. If the congregation has a copy of the program, little more needs to be said.
8) Don't read the printed announcements unless you need to correct or clarify something in the bulletin.

USHER

Edwin Hayden, former editor of *Christian Standard*, once observed, "Leading a visitor to a seat in the place of worship may be an important first step in leading him to Christ." Trained and sensitive ushers can do a great deal to help guests feel welcome, services run smoothly, and participants concentrate on their part in the worship. An usher should arrive early, secure bulletins, and check the lights and ventilation. His appropriate dress combined with his relaxed and friendly spirit help to make the visitor feel welcome immediately.

"Leading a visitor to a seat in the place of worship may be an important first step in leading him to Christ."

Serving as an usher is an excellent way for new church leaders to minister. By doing this they become acquainted with the congregation and the mechanics of the service, and they render a valuable ministry at the same time. A proper sense of decorum and a concern for making the worshiper feel comfortable are the keys to success in this work. As one person observed, "Ushers must not be civic club backslappers with loud voices nor mum funeral parlor robots."

In whatever ways the church leader may be asked to serve in the public eye, he will do well to remember that his first responsibility is to the Lord. Paul's counsel applies here: "Whatever you do, work at it with all your heart, as working for the Lord, not for men" (Colossians 3:23).

Becoming More Effective

Through Action:

Practice reading Scripture aloud and then do so in a service; try giving a brief devotional talk or meditation before a class or small group.

Through Reading:

Bell, Buddy. *Greeting 101.* Tulsa: Harrison House, 1998.

Johnson, Alvin D. *Work of the Usher.* Valley Forge, PA: Judson, 1991.

Miller, Herb. *Leadership Is the Key: Unlocking Your Effectiveness in Ministry.* Nashville: Abingdon, 1997.

Thomas, Gary. *Sacred Pathways: Discover Your Soul's Path to God.* Grand Rapids: Zondervan, 2000.

Questions to Ponder

1. How can a shy person begin taking a more visible role in church activities?

2. Do you remember the television show of years past, "Candid Camera"? What would be a time and place that you most certainly would *not* want to be "caught" on "Candid Camera"?

3. Do you believe that who we are when no one is looking is who we really are? Does what a church leader does in private have any ramifications on his public ministry?

4. There will always be a nervousness that accompanies church leaders when they speak in front of the congregation. What are are a few reminders or tips for maintaining your confidence when serving in the spotlight?

5. It's been said, "You never get a second chance to make a good first impression." With this in mind, how important are the roles of greeters, ushers, and worship service participants? Should church leaders invest time and energy into training individuals in the church for these roles?

6. What are several service options you would suggest for the shy person in your church?

Looking Ahead:

Many of the leader's activities are done in the spotlight. A far greater number are done behind the scenes. The leader will many times serve in ways that will receive no recognition. How important is it for the church leader to feel confident in his relationship with God? Take a few minutes to meditate on the following "confidence-building" Scriptures that remind us of our standing in Christ Jesus: John 15:15; 1 Corinthians 6:20; Ephesians 1:5; 2:18; Colossians 1:14; 2:10; Philippians 1:6; 3:20; 4:13; and 2 Timothy 1:7.

DOES ANYONE NOTICE?

In this chapter:
✔ Know your flock
✔ Support the staff in every way possible
✔ Serve those in need without thought of recognition

At times you will feel conspicuous by being in front of others, but at other times you will wonder if anyone knows or cares about the behind-the-scenes work you are doing.

Like the iceberg with only a small fraction appearing above the ocean's surface, the church leader does the greater part of his work away from the spotlight of public attention.

Accepting this truth is crucial for a leader.

Some want recognition. They want to be seen. If they are not noticed, praised, and thanked for their work, they get their feelings hurt. Both the teaching and the life of Jesus demonstrate that true greatness comes through service. When you work for Him without thought of reward, you help demonstrate your suitability to be a Christian leader. An elder, for example, is instructed to shepherd or pastor the flock (see Acts 20:28; 1 Peter 5:2). This is not primarily done by standing before them in a public service. It involves personal involvement with people, often on a one-to-one basis.

> *When you work for Him without thought of reward, you help demonstrate your suitability to be a Christian leader.*

CALLING IN THE HOME

Those who attempt to shepherd must know their flock. The sheep must know their voice. No better way has been found to enhance this relationship than informal time shared in the home of the leader or the member.

To call on a person—especially at first—can be a traumatic experience. Callers need encouragement. One new worker was quite shy, so the preacher told him, "You'll find it helpful if you spend a few moments talking to God before you make the call." When the callers came back to report, the timid one came directly to the preacher.

He said enthusiastically, "Thank you for what you said about prayer. I tried it when I went on my call—and it works."

"I'm glad to hear that," beamed the preacher. "Tell us what happened."

"Well, I prayed the people wouldn't be home, and they weren't!"

Training leaders to call on prospects or members need not be difficult. After going over some basic principles, the ideal way for one to learn to call is to go out with an experienced caller.

Taking someone with you is always an excellent practice that has biblical precedent (Matthew 10). When the church leader and his wife go into a home together, they remove a number of potential problems that could arise if he were to go alone. A second person is not only a witness of all that was said and done, but the person may also help care for children or pets. The other person can also pray and add testimony and encouragement.

By calling on members, the church leader can make a valuable contribution to the kingdom. He learns about the attitudes and needs of those in his flock. He sees them "on their own turf." They can talk freely and frankly. He can teach, listen, read the Bible, and pray with them, depending on the need.

SUPPORT THE CHURCH STAFF

One of the important tasks of a local church leader is to provide counsel and encouragement to the paid staff members. The minister may be the only person in the congregation who has no minister.

The minister may be the only person in the congregation who has no minister.

You can begin by praying for him. When my son, Jeff, began his first ministry after Bible college, the sensitive and loving church leaders there gave them a special beginning.

The elders and the minister met with Jeff and Johnnie in the minister's office. The elders talked first to her. "Johnnie, we want you to know that we hired Jeff today—not you. We realize your first responsibility is to help take care of Jeff and minister to him, so that he can minister with the church. We're not thinking that we are hiring two people for one salary!" Then they told Jeff of their joy at his coming and assured him of their support.

One elder said, "We want to cover you both with our prayers now. This will be a busy time for you and it's an important step for all of us." With that, the elders joined hands and formed a circle around Jeff and Johnnie. Each one prayed aloud for the young minister and his wife.

What a wonderful way to begin a ministry! Prayers are needed throughout. Just as Aaron and Hur held up the hands of Moses (Exodus 17:12), so the leaders of the church need to uphold their preacher and other leaders in prayer.

A leader can encourage the staff members to take their day off each week, to spend time with their families, and to enjoy vacations. No one can be "on call" twenty-four hours a day, seven days a week. Understanding and support will help church staff members do an even better job in their ministry.

Minor problems should be handled without bothering the preacher. Responsible elders can care for many duties and decisions without involving the minister. Working deacons can function actively in service projects needing minimal input from him.

Thoughtfulness in remembering birthdays and anniversaries of the staff will certainly be appreciated. Noting their anniversary of service with the local church will, too! Such fringe benefits as assistance with continuing education, adequate health insurance, and a retirement program will help the staff members give themselves more fully and adequately to their ministry.

Expressing gratitude to everyone—staff, coworker, or member—is a healthy trait to develop. Some years ago we worshiped with a congregation in Indiana. During the morning service, the preacher said, "Now the elders have an announcement to make." My thoughts raced ahead. What could this be? Is there a problem in the church? Does some difficulty exist? Are the members upset about something?

The smiling chairman of the elders stepped forward. "On behalf of the elders," he began, "I just want to thank all of you ladies who did such a wonderful job in preparing the meal for our area men's fellowship last week." He went on to tell how much the elders appreciated the cooperative attitude and willing spirit of all of the congregation.

As he returned to his seat, my thoughts wandered off again. How long has it been since the elders in other churches have taken a moment to express publicly their appreciation for some helpful service rendered by various members? Perhaps it's time to do it at your church, too.

HELPING OTHERS

Loving service to others is a characteristic of Jesus' disciples. It is essential for church leaders. Scripture judges only servant leaders as worthy to lead the Lord's church. "Whoever wants to become great among you must be your servant, and whoever wants to be first must be your slave—just as the Son of Man did not come to be served, but to serve, and to give his life as a ransom for many" (Matthew 20:26-28).

Loving service to others is a characteristic of Jesus' disciples.

Help can come in many ways. If you have trouble thinking of some, read Romans 12. Then make a list of possibilities. You'll find such things as

- Rejoicing with those who rejoice
- Weeping with those who weep
- Practicing hospitality
- Contributing to the needs of others
- Sharing with those in need

Jesus is our example. The Bible says, "He went around doing good." So often we are content simply to go around.

Taking food to someone who is sick, calling at the funeral home, sending a note to a lonely soldier or college student, driving a senior citizen to the doctor, mowing the lawn at church—there is no end to the good things we can do. Most of them will probably be unnoticed and unrecognized by the church in general. But Jesus will see. His promise holds true: "Whatever you did for one of the least of these brothers of mine, you did for me" (Matthew 25:40). "Your Father, who sees what is done in secret, will reward you" (Matthew 6:6).

Becoming More Effective

Through Action:

Act out a typical call in which one makes a friendly, get-acquainted visit on a person who has visited the church. Then discuss how to improve the approach used in such a visit.

Through Reading:

Faust, David. *Taking Truth Next Door.* Cincinnati: Standard Publishing, 1999.

Fulenwider, Ray. *The Servant-driven Church.* Joplin, MO: College Press, 1998.

Pierson, Jim. *Exceptional Teaching: A Comprehensive Guide for Including Students with Disabilities.* Cincinnati: Standard Publishing, 2002.

Stone, Dave. *I'd Rather See a Sermon: Showing Your Friends the Way to Heaven.* Rev. Ed. Joplin, MO: College Press, 2000.

Questions to Ponder

1. Do you believe that the most important thing in life is *relationships*—first, our vertical relationship with God and then our horizontal relationships with other human beings? Why do you agree or disagree?

2. What are the advantages of going calling two-by-two?

3. Ministry *is* people. People of all types and personalities—some easy to get along with, others, well, not so easy. What are some of the critical "people skills" for the church leader to possess?

4. Do you think people are more receptive or less receptive to home visits today than they were a few decades ago? What can be done to make families feel at ease and actually look forward to church leaders "calling" on them?

5. How do you view your minister (or ministers in a multistaff church)? Is he a hired employee only, or is he considered a member of the leadership team, part of the family?

6. What are several ways you can encourage and support your minister(s)?

7. What are some "acts of kindness" that your church has done in the past? What are your ideas for future projects in your community?

Looking Ahead:

Never doubt that a small group of committed people can change the world. Jesus called twelve, not thousands or millions. Those twelve followers, ignited by a common vision, united as a team and "turned the world upside down" (Acts 17:6b, KJV). Just how important is unity and working together as a team? Will a church be more or less effective when the leaders unite and serve as a team? The upcoming chapter will focus on the necessity of leaders working together as a team.

HOW CAN WE WORK TOGETHER?

In this chapter:

✔ An understanding of who is under whose authority is essential
✔ The church leadership should be a family of understanding, love, and concern
✔ Leaders should be given respect from the congregation

Teamwork is the key to success in the local church. Under Christ, capable leaders with varying talents blend their efforts in order to accomplish the Lord's purposes.

These leaders must not only work with other leaders, though, but with paid staff and with the entire congregation as well. The preacher, leaders, and congregation must work together in harmony for the work of the

Teamwork is the key to success in the local church.

church to be successful. You need both an understanding of church polity and a desire to demonstrate a Christlike spirit.

AUTHORITY

Among the three, the congregation must retain final authority. The elders are selected by the members and are answerable to them. The church must follow the leadership of the elders as long as they are elders. Elders are not infallible, however. They may make mistakes. A man may prove to be unsuitable for the task. The congregation has recourse to remove a man who is unfit, unable, or unwilling to function.

The example of the New Testament is that a plurality of elders should direct the affairs of the church (Acts 14:23). They are scripturally commissioned to "be shepherds of God's flock that is under your care" (1 Peter 5:2). The elder is called an overseer; he is to care for God's church just as a man would manage his own household (1 Timothy 3:5).

The evangelist is not to be a dictator who runs roughshod over the feelings of the congregation. While some use Titus 1:5 as a directive for the evangelist alone to "appoint elders" in every town, proper interpretation does not support this view. The same word that is used for "appoint" in this text is used in Acts 6. In that case, the people selected men for positions of responsibility; then the apostles "appointed" them—that is they set them apart to the work with prayer and the laying on of hands. Even though in a new congregation the evangelist might suggest potential elders to the congregation, the Lord's people have a responsibility to select those whom they are going to follow.

No minister should feel that he is above the authority of the elders. The writer of Hebrews put it this way: "Obey your leaders and submit to their authority. They keep watch over you as men who must give an account" (Hebrews 13:17). The minister, like every other member, is under the oversight of the elders within a local congregation.

While this is true, it does not mean that the minister is subservient like a slave to a taskmaster. He may better be compared to an executive carrying out the policies of a board of directors. Naturally his counsel will be sought, his advice gratefully received, and his experience appreciated. He is a part of the leadership team. In some congregations, the minister is elected to serve as an elder—since he is expected to help shepherd the flock. Others do not follow this practice. It would be arbitrary to make a judgment that either arrangement is always the best.

> *No minister should feel that he is above the authority of the elders.*

When a new preacher is contacted by the elders (and it seems obvious that they should be the pulpit committee), he can assess their ability and aptitude just as they will consider his. It is of paramount importance that complete honesty and trust undergird every relationship of the minister and the elders. Nothing less is good enough.

The church leaders should take particular concern for the well-being of the minister and his family. They need the assurance that they can call on someone for help when they need it.

It is necessary to distinguish between the roles of elder and deacon. The elders are the church leaders. They should make the primary decisions of the congregation (not simply "spiritual" matters). The deacons are helpers. They are to assist in the ministry of the church fulfilling various duties assigned them by the elders.

A well-informed, well-taught congregation will rejoice to see the minister and the elders leading the church with love and unity. Such harmony needs to be the goal of every group of believers.

RELATIONSHIPS

Few passages in the New Testament provide the insights into the proper relationship between the preacher and other church leaders as does Acts 20:17-28. Three characteristics are seen in that text. First, it suggests that the preacher and the elders were *known to each other*. Many think that Paul did his most outstanding work at Ephesus. During his three years there, multitudes of the Diana worshipers were converted and many involved in the occult gave their lives to Jesus (Acts 19). Paul had lived alongside the brethren. He knew the elders; they knew him.

They had labored together through difficult circumstances. When individuals share in work, weariness, or worry, they come to understand each other better and to love each other more.

These elders had heard and tested Paul's teaching. They had watched him. And he had watched them. With inspired vision, he warned, "I know that after I leave, savage wolves will come in among you and will not spare the flock. Even from your own number men will arise and distort the truth in order to draw away disciples after them" (Acts 20:29,30). Paul knew their weaknesses as well as their strengths.

This knowledge was not a one-way street. "When they arrived, he said to them: 'You know how I lived the whole time I was with you, from the first day I came into the province of Asia'" (v. 18). He could speak openly of his attitude and his actions because they knew that he was speaking the truth. He was able to say, "I have not hesitated to proclaim to you the whole will of God" (v. 27). What a goal for every gospel preacher! What an ideal toward which an elder should strive!

Paul and the Ephesian elders had something more in common—they were also *loved by each other*. Unfortunately this harmonious spirit does not always exist. One minister was seriously ill. An elder came to see him. He leaned over and whispered, "Preacher, I wanted you to know that the elders just met and we voted five to three to pray for your recovery."

In the Ephesian church, relationships were different. All of the elders loved Paul and he loved them. He wanted to see them, and they had walked some thirty miles to see him. Paul viewed the church like a flock of sheep needing these men as shepherds (v. 28); he wept over them (v. 31); he prayed for them (v. 32); he cared about them.

Love builds churches. The late T.K. Smith, for years minister with First Christian Church, Columbus, Indiana, advised a group of preachers, "Here is a challenge to every minister young or old. Would you succeed? Then love thy people. Love them so completely that nothing keeps you from a ministry of unrestricted service to them."

As Paul and his friends prepared to part, their love was demonstrated by their tears and warm embrace. When the preacher and the elders do not seek their own way, are not easily provoked, think no evil, and do not rejoice in iniquity, love abounds (1 Corinthians 13). Such a spirit ensures that all concerned will bear, believe, hope, and endure whatever comes.

Moreover, these church leaders were *concerned for each other.* For those whom one knows and loves, this is natural.

Paul cautioned, "So be on your guard!" (v. 31). Eternal vigilance is still the price of liberty. When a preacher leaves a congregation, he remains concerned for its future. Babes in Christ need food; young Christians need nurture; older saints need attention and help. True shepherds may be distinguished from hirelings by their concern for the flock (John 10:1-15).

The apostle encouraged the church leaders, "Now I commit you to God and to the word of his grace, which can build you up and give you an inheritance among all those who are sanctified" (Acts 20:32).

F.F. Bruce described the scene like this:

> Now he was leaving them; they could no longer count upon his personal presence for such pastoral guidance and wise admonition. But, though Paul might go, God was ever with them, and so was God's Word which they had received—the word that proclaimed His grace in redeeming them and His grace in sanctifying them. To God, then, and to this word of His, Paul solemnly committed them (*The Book of Acts* [Grand Rapids: Eerdmans, 1994]).

The preacher and elders prayed together (Acts 20:36). This demonstrates concern even as it builds concern. In some churches, the minister and elders meet together regularly for a time of prayer in addition to their "business sessions."

When they heard that Paul had been warned of bonds and afflictions awaiting him, they were sad. But when he told them that he did not expect to see their faces again (Acts 20:25), this was too much. They sorrowed. "What grieved them most was his statement that they would never see his face again. Then they accompanied him to the ship" (Acts 20:38).

Blessed is the church where the preacher and the church leaders are known to each other, loved by each other, and are concerned for each other. In fact, this is the kind of family relationship that should exist among all in the local assembly of believers.

RESPECT

Besides following their direction, the congregation has some definite responsibilities for helping their leaders work better. Most preachers seem to concentrate on sermons about the qualifications or the duties of elders and deacons. But when did you hear a message outlining the congregation's obligations to their leaders?

Give them recognition. Many congregations fail to say "thank you" as they should—not only to leaders, but to those who sing, teach, and serve in a myriad of other ways. The biblical principle is that those who serve well are to be honored. "Give everyone what you owe him . . . if respect, then respect; if honor, then honor" (Romans 13:7). "The elders who direct the affairs of the church well are worthy of double honor, especially those whose work is preaching and teaching" (1 Timothy 5:17).

Elders are to be the spiritual rulers of the church—not in a proud, arrogant way, lording it over others, but as a shepherd lovingly and carefully watches out for his sheep. Elders who serve well in this role are deserving of double honor, especially those who exercise the gift of public instruction. Paul suggests that those who give their full-time efforts in Christian leadership jobs should be supported by the church they serve (1 Corinthians 9:1-14).

The church should provide a fair wage for those who are employed by them. Christians should see that this principle finds its fullest application to all in Christian service—not only full-time elders, but those who teach in a Bible college, work on the mission field, or serve in other capacities in the church.

An experienced Christian leader wisely observed that, in addition to meeting the financial needs, there are little things we can do that mean a lot to others such as recognizing their anniversaries and birthdays, and giving gifts at Christmas. These little attentions have double value. They help others to feel appreciated and bring joy into their lives, and a happy worker is the best worker. They also elevate the position of the worker in the eyes of the people so that they value his or her leadership.

A church will become no greater than its leaders. If your congregation is blessed with capable and dedicated leaders, let them know of your appreciation and support. Long hours and sacrificial service become easier when one receives an occasional word of thanks.

> *A church will become no greater than its leaders.*

Protect their reputation. Paul wrote, "Do not entertain an accusation against an elder unless it is brought by two or three witnesses" (1 Timothy 5:19).

A Christian should be cautious in receiving any accusation against a spiritual leader in the church. It is of utmost importance to safeguard innocent people from false accusation. The Jewish law required the agreement of two witnesses before a man might be called upon to answer a charge. So it must be in the church—especially when that person is an elder.

It is always easy to criticize. It is always easy to follow that dangerous exercise of jumping to conclusions. Some people can make up their minds about a case without bothering to investigate the truth. Their minds are like concrete, all mixed up and permanently set. We must not be like that. When someone comes to you with a rumor, a piece of gossip, an accusation about an elder or other church leader, don't be quick to believe it. Leaders should be protected from malicious intent or ignorant charges.

And yet, Paul says, on the other hand, if there are real grounds for the accusation, then disciplinary action must be taken before the whole church. "Those who sin are to be rebuked publicly, so that the others may take warning" (v. 20). This policy is also for protecting the reputation both of the other leaders and of the church. It involves those who "persist in sin" and the purpose of it is "that the rest may stand in fear." Let people know that it means something to be a Christian leader. Let the community know that the church expects something from its leaders. The office of a church leader is not a favor to be granted, nor an award to be given—it is a serious, God-ordained position of leadership that calls for men to be examples.

What Paul told Timothy might well apply to any church leader: "Set an example for the believers in speech, in life, in love, in faith and in purity" (1 Timothy 4:12).

Becoming More Effective

Through Action:

Reread the pastoral epistles (1 and 2 Timothy and Titus), making notes about what leaders and followers are to do; and/or plan a recognition/appreciation service for leaders in the local church.

Through Reading:

Armour, Michael C., and Don Browning. *Systems-Sensitive Leadership: Empowering Diversity without Polarizing the Church.* Rev. Ed. Joplin, MO: College Press, 2000.

Gangel, Kenneth. *Team Leadership in Christian Ministry.* Chicago: Moody, 1997.

Greenleaf, Robert J. *A Journey into the Nature of Legitimate Power and Greatness.* Mahwah, NJ: Paulist Press, 1977.

Russell, Bob and Rusty. *When God Builds a Church: 10 Principles for Growing a Dynamic Church—The Remarkable Story of Southeast Christian Church.* West Monroe, LA: Howard, 2000. (Note especially chapters 3 and 6.)

Questions to Ponder

1. Do you remember from your past being on a successful team of some sort (e.g., athletic, musical, or dramatic)? What were a few of the contributing factors to your team's success?

2. Why do you think the Bible reveals that the early church was led by a "plurality" of elders?

3. A football team has a quarterback, a band has a drum major, a company has a CEO and the church of Jesus Christ has a _____ (how would you fill in the blank?).

4. When it comes to accountability, who is accountable to whom in the leadership structure of the local church—the minister to the elders, the elders to the minister, or both?

5. We read that the church leaders should "take particular concern for the well-being of the minister and his family." What are some ways your church is already accomplishing this objective? What are some ideas to improve on encouraging and supporting your minister?

6. What are some ways for the ministers and elders to build better, closer relationships? We read about Paul and the Ephesian elders praying together (Acts 20). Do the leaders of your church meet regularly for this express purpose of lifting one another and the needs of the church family up in prayer?

7. Make it a goal to target one church leader each week for you to send an encouraging note or to give a genuine word of encouragement (either face-to-face on a Sunday morning or via the telephone).

Looking Ahead:

Many churches suffer morale setbacks when they spend too much time and energy looking inward instead of outward. Our Lord Jesus instructed us to maintain a God-centered vision for engaging in world evangelization (Matthew 28:18-20). In the next chapter, we will be challenged to turn up the volume on the passion of our world evangelism intensity. How's your worldview? How much time have you personally invested lately in praying for the world's harvest fields?

11

WHAT'S HAPPENING OUT THERE?

In this chapter:
✔ Understand the responsibility the church has to the rest of the world
✔ Develop leadership potential in the youth and other members of your church
✔ Allow your staff to participate in programs outside your congregation; participate yourself if possible

A church wrapped up in itself makes a small package—too small, in fact. Christ commissioned His disciples to win the world for Him (Matthew 28:18-20). If you are to be a leader in the local congregation. you must develop a "kingdom view."

It is not enough to decide "what is best for us" only for your local congregation. The church leader must try to see every decision in light of the church's mission. For this reason, many churches are attempting to write a mission statement. Then all choices—including budget distribution, staff priorities, and programming emphasis—are tested in light of this statement.

Unfortunately some church leaders are like the fellow whose friend was telling him about a speaker on television. "The guy was great," his friend declared. "He said that all the world's problems could be reduced to two things—ignorance and apathy. What do you think of that?"

A church wrapped up in itself makes a small package—too small, in fact.

The fellow replied, "I don't know and I don't care."

Too many people seem to feel that way!

Every person and every church is tempted to be satisfied with what we are doing for others. We all are prone to "look out for number one." "Charity begins at home," we explain. We want to be sure that we are okay. Then whatever is left, whatever we can spare, whatever we didn't want anyway—that can be given to others.

One poet described a life that never sees beyond its own doorstep.

> I had a little tea party
> This afternoon at three.
> 'Twas very small,
> Three guests in all—
> Just I, myself, and me.
> Myself ate all the sandwiches,
> While I drank up the tea;
> 'Twas also I who ate the pie
> And passed the cake to me.

The verse can also apply to a church that does not reach out beyond its own comfort and convenience. Biblically qualified leaders want something better. They want to direct the local church out of the comfort zone of easy Christianity—into the challenge and thrill of trusting Jesus and following Him, wherever He may lead. Here are some ways the leader can encourage this:

BE COMMITTED TO WORLD EVANGELISM

The mission of the church involves evangelism and nurture, winning souls to Christ both at home and abroad. The early church left a spider web of mission trails across the world. But what of us?

Statisticians estimate that if the world population were scaled down to be represented by one thousand people, sixty would be Americans, yet these would possess half the wealth. Five hundred would never have heard of Christ. All of the denominations of Christianity would number three hundred thirty with fewer than one hundred considered Protestant. How will those who hunger for the bread of life find it, unless we offer it to them? How will our family, friends, and neighbors come to know Christ unless we are sufficiently convinced that we must share our faith with them?

Missions is not just a committee in the church.

Missions is not just a committee in the church—it represents the task of the church. Our mind-set must include the need for community outreach, the desire to start new congregations, and the willingness to send and support those who will go to other areas.

Many churches pray the "Lord's Prayer" as a part of their regular worship services. As long as the participants mean what they are saying, that is fine. But what about the prayer that Jesus commanded us to pray? How often do we pray it? Jesus told His followers, "The harvest is plentiful, but the workers are few. Ask the Lord of the harvest, therefore, to send out workers into his harvest field" (Luke 10:2).

RECRUIT WORKERS

How long has it been since a young person from your church was ordained to Christian ministry or missionary service? How many from your congregation are now attending a Bible college or seminary? Leaders need to ask themselves three questions:

1) *Are we encouraging our young people to enter a specialized Christian service?* The fields are still "white unto harvest." The laborers are still too few. What are we doing to help our young people discern the need, develop their talents, and dedicate their lives to the Lord?

A visitor asked an older deacon at one church, "Have you produced many preachers at this congregation?"

"Nope," the man replied, "but we've used up a heap of 'em!"

Unless we challenge our youth, the church will lack leadership in the years ahead.

All too many churches would have to say the same thing. Unless we challenge our finest youth to consider God's claim upon their lives, the church will lack leadership in the years ahead.

2) *Are we keeping in contact with those we have ordained?* When the elders lay hands on a minister and set him apart to do a special work, their responsibility is not over; it has just begun. They must maintain periodic contact with those men they ordain—supporting the discouraged, giving praise for good works, and correcting those who have erred. An eldership that ordains a man to the ministry is responsible for him just as he is responsible to them.

Elders may well follow a practice of regular, periodic contact with their "Timothys." This not only can be a source of encouragement both to the preacher and the church but it can also provide a doctrinal and moral "checkup" for the minister. Regardless of just how it is done and whether such contact is initiated by the minister or the elders, the two should keep in touch.

3) *Are we checking with the ordaining church when we consider a prospective minister?* In looking for a new minister, a pulpit committee should always contact the elders of the candidate's ordaining church. These men can evaluate the minister's strengths and weaknesses and report on his work through the years. Such routine inquiry can protect a church from an individual who might be potentially harmful to it.

If each Christian leader will ask these three questions, good will result.

We ought to recruit our finest young men and women for the gospel ministry. Opportunities for training and service within the local church can be enhanced by continuing, specialized study in Bible college and seminary.

Elders must accept their responsibilities in ordaining only those who are duly and Scripturally qualified. Those workers they do ordain deserve their prayers, their support, their discipline, and their love.

SHARE YOUR PREACHER

In self-governing churches, it is especially important that leaders support cooperative efforts beyond the local congregation. The church is broader than the community of believers who worship in our meeting house. Realization of this fact will help prevent provincialism and encourage expansion of the kingdom.

Your preacher will frequently have opportunities to participate in various phases of brotherhood life. Camps, benevolent works, new church evangelism, conventions, Bible colleges, and other missions will need his help. For his services he will usually receive no more than an occasional meal or mileage check. Such participation is a part of his ministry. The local church must support him in it.

The church is broader than the community of believers in our meeting house.

It is unfair for a church to send its young people to a Christian service camp, for example, and not furnish any of the volunteer leadership for the camp program. It is not right to send our young people to Bible college and never assist in the program of the school. The principle applies to conventions and mission works as well. Someone must spend the time to see that these beneficial programs succeed. While none of us can help with them all, all can help with some.

Many needs of groups and programs beyond the local church may be supplied by members other than the paid staff. Frequently, however, the time or place for a given task rules out those who have full-time jobs elsewhere. In such situations the local church leadership must encourage the preacher's participation.

A preacher should not become so involved with activities outside the local church that he fails to do his job at home. But if each church shares its leadership, no local program need suffer. All will be helping with the work of the church at large.

One caution should be given to the minister as he becomes involved in work beyond his community: keep your motives pure. Do not look on such participation as a way to become known by influential people or as a chance to exert power. Such concepts are directly opposed to the teaching of our Lord.

Real success comes from obedience to Him through service to others.

Real success comes from obedience to Him through service to others (Matthew 20:20-28). For that purpose, church leaders, share your preacher!

Becoming More Effective

Through Action:

Interview a missionary supported by the church and ask for suggestions on ways to involve the members more closely with his work.

Through Reading:

Bowland, Terry. *Make Disciples! Reaching the Postmodern World for Christ.* Joplin, MO: College Press, 1999.

Callahan, K.L. *Effective Church Leadership.* New York: Harper & Row, 1983.

Walter, Darren. *The People-Magnet Church: Attracting Your Community to Christ.* Joplin, MO: College Press, 2001.

Warren, Rick. *The Purpose-Driven Church.* Grand Rapids: Zondervan, 1996. (This is also available in cassette format from Zondervan Audio Pages.)

Questions to Ponder

1. Is your congregation giving adequate concern to world evangelism? Does your church budget reflect what you say your priorities are?

2. Are you aware of the missions your local church supports? Who could you call to find out more information about them? Make an effort this week to learn more about your church's worldwide outreach.

3. Do you agree that "all the world's problems could be reduced to two things — ignorance and apathy"?

4. Does your church have a "mission statement"? If so, how prominent a place does world missions have in that mission? If your church doesn't have one, who could you encourage this next week to begin the process of formulating one?

5. What was your answer to the thought-provoking questions in this chapter? Are we encouraging young people to enter a specialized Christian service? Are we keeping in contact with those we have ordained? Are we checking with the ordaining church when we consider a prospective minister?

6. Is the leadership of your church apt to encourage or discourage your preacher from accepting outside speaking opportunities?

7. Are short-term missions trips an annual event in the life of your church? What could be done to involve more of your members in missions?

Looking Ahead:

Leaders and followers need each other. Just as the word "right" makes no sense without "left," leader and follower go together. In fact, leadership and followership cannot be separated. Your followership sets the pattern for your leadership in the Lord's church. What kind of a *follower* are you? Ponder the following quotes as you prepare to read the final chapter: "If you wanna be top banana, you gotta start at the bottom of the bunch" (Comedian, Phil Silvers). "Who would learn to lead must first of all learn to obey" (Aristotle).

12

WHO'S LEADING WHOM?

In this chapter:
✔ The need for qualified, scriptural leaders
✔ Learning to lead by learning to follow

Every leader must first be a follower. Even when you lead in some settings, you will follow in others. All church leaders must follow Jesus. Those who follow leaders in the local congregation should do so only as far as those leaders are following Christ (see 1 Corinthians 11:1).

All church leaders must follow Jesus.

The Christian Leadership Letter published by World Vision devoted an entire issue to the theme, "Followership" (September, 1986).

In the ongoing search for the definition of a leader, the best we have been able to do is to define a leader as "A person who has followers in a given situation."
. . . We are all leaders in some things. We are followers in others. . . .

The very qualities that the Bible defines for good leaders apply almost equally to good followers. The secular world seems to have learned this lesson well. The good commanding officer is one who has learned what it means to be a good follower. The effective executive leader is the one who has learned to serve his or her boss well. The popular phrase "servant leadership" recognizes that those who have learned to serve (follow) others are those who make the best leaders.

Those of us who lead in the church must also be willing to follow. We will not be "in authority" or prominent in every Christian activity and project. Nor should we be. At times all of us will be under the direction of others.

This is healthy. In the Master's kingdom, none are to seek position and power; all are to desire submission and service. By our acceptance of proper authority, we demonstrate to those who follow us what biblical leadership entails.

When Standard Publishing announced the "Year of the Leader" emphasis, a young missionary objected. He quoted Matthew 23:11—"The greatest among you will be your servant." Then he asked, "Why not have the year of the servant? We don't need leaders."

The fact is we do need them. The Bible says so. Furthermore, the Word commands our respect for and responsiveness to their leadership. "Obey your leaders and submit to their authority. They keep watch over you as men who must give an account," the writer of Hebrews declared (Hebrews 13:17).

Having leaders is proper and scriptural. But they must be properly qualified leaders who lead in a scriptural way. They not only must have followers, but also other leaders who will encourage, support, and counsel them.

Dr. Robert Schuller asked, "What else does a leader need? A fellowship of positive people. When possibility thinkers and believers encourage each other and dare to accept encouragement, wonderful things happen. But it takes courage and humility to accept encouragement, to ask someone to pray for you, to say, 'I need some help and support.' Leaders need other leaders to nudge them in the right direction."

The only ones who are recognized as leaders by Christ are those who have first learned to be servants. Our Lord made clear that the "chief seats" are not for those who climb over others in their rush to get the top. Instead they are reserved for those who don't worry about status, but are content to serve, however menial the task (Matthew 20:20-28).

Truly great people are also humble. The famous Philippine statesman, Carlos P. Romulo, told of a saying in his country, "The taller the bamboo grows, the lower it bends."

The name "Mother Teresa" has become synonymous with sacrificial service in the world today. Ted Engstrom observed that the world has normally rejected the concept of servant leadership that this remarkable woman exem-

Truly great people are also humble.

plified. Yet with the sole intention in her lifetime of serving Jesus by serving the poorest of the poor, the late Mother Teresa has gained the following of millions. This is the paradox of servant leadership.

Every leader must also be a follower. Those who claim Jesus as Lord must demonstrate that they are following Him before they can expect others to follow them. Then, as we yield our talents to Him, we find that He can bless and multiply them to accomplish His purpose.

Such a spirit helps guard one from the danger of seeking power. Leaders in a local church must guard against demonstrating any supposed authority in a reckless or high-handed manner. Peter explained clearly the way in which leaders are to lead. He told the elders, "Be shepherds of God's flock that is under your care, serving as overseers—not because you must, but because you are willing, as God wants you to be; . . . not lording it over those entrusted to you, but being examples to the flock" (1 Peter 5:2,3).

Author Ray S. Anderson said that servant leadership is essentially a gifted leadership rather than a self-serving leadership. It is a calling and gift to exemplify the life of Christ, who gave himself for the church, His body. The vision of leadership thus comes from above to below, from promise to practice.

Dr. Jess Moody, a popular preacher and writer, enjoys telling about a "Meeting of the Tools" that helps put this in perspective. The meeting went like this:

Mr. Hammer was presiding. Brother Screwdriver said, "Brother Hammer must go because he is always making noise, always knocking."

Hammer said, "Brother Screwdriver has to go because you have to turn him around all the time to get him to do his job."

Someone else said, "Brother Plane has to go. He always wants to just touch the surface. He never goes deep."

Plane said, "Brother Sandpaper has to go then because he is always rubbing people the wrong way."

Sandpaper spoke up, "Then Brother Saw must go because he is always cutting things up and leaving sawdust all over the place."

Then the Carpenter of Nazareth came in. "I need all of you. We have a job to do. Put yourselves in my hand. Let me use you."

Hammer said, "Here am I, Lord, use me." Screwdriver said, "Here am I, Lord, use me." Plane said, "Here am I, Lord, use me." Sandpaper said, "Here am I, Lord, use me." Saw said, "Here am I, Lord, use me."

So when each gave himself to the Carpenter from Nazareth together they built:

1. A church in which the gospel could be preached.
2. A bridge of understanding so differing groups could get together.
3. A house so that a home could be built.
4. A coffin to bury Satan in.

That is what happens when all the tools are put in the Carpenter's hands and are used for the purpose for which they were made.

Christ is our ultimate leader. He alone is worthy of our complete allegiance.

If the Christian leader is seeking first of all to follow Jesus, he will not be concerned about what other leaders on earth he may need to follow—nor about how many people are following him. Instead he will seek to be faithful to his responsibility, submitting to the head of the church and seeking to obey His will faithfully every day.

Christ is our ultimate leader. He alone is worthy of our complete allegiance. An African native put it beautifully—"Lord, You be the needle and I'll be the thread. I'll follow wherever You lead."

Becoming More Effective

Through Action:

Secure follow-up help for continuing growth in church leadership. Try one or more of these ideas:

1. View a video presentation on some aspect of church leadership. Helpful messages are available by outstanding Christian teachers (such as Alan Ahlgrim, Alger Fitch, Ben Merold, and Woodrow Phillips) from Good News Productions, International. You may contact them at P.O. Box 222, Joplin, MO 64802; phone (800) 457-4674.

2. Workshop outlines and manuscripts from the North American Christian Convention are available each year after the annual meeting. For information, check the NACC Web site (**www.nacc-online.org**) or write to the Convention at 110 Boggs Lane, Suite 330, Cincinnati, OH 45246.

3. Select one of the resource books suggested in this study and use it as the basis for a follow-up class or personal development.

Through Reading:

Habecker, Eugene B. *Leading with a Follower's Heart.* Wheaton, IL: Victor, 1990.

Jones, Laurie Beth. *Jesus, Inc.* New York: Hyperion, 2001.

Stowell, Joseph M. *Shepherding the Church into the 21st Century.* Wheaton: Victor Books, 1994.

Sweet, Leonard. *AquaChurch: Essential Leadership Arts for Piloting Your Church in Today's Fluid Culture.* Loveland, CO: Group Publishing, 1999.

Questions to Ponder

1. The Apostle Paul issues the stunning challenge, "Follow my example, as I follow the example of Christ" (1 Cor. 11:1, NIV). Could you honestly say that you are diligently following the example of Christ to the extent that you could ask others to follow *your* example?

2. Leaders must in some cases be followers. What are some instances in your church where the leaders are placed in "follower" positions? If there is a leader who is extremely reluctant to follow, what should be done with this individual?

3. Humility is one of the most necessary qualities in the life of a leader. Is it a quality that can be "learned"? What are some ways this quality can be developed?

4. What are some ways that local church leaders could be regularly reminded of their need to submit fully to the leadership of the head of the church—our Lord Jesus Christ? Would annual retreats be enough? Monthly prayer meetings? Weekly accountability meetings?

Internet Resources for Ongoing Help:

Many Web sites provide useful and practical help for Christian leaders. Following are a few of them:

Best of the Christian Web: **www.botcw.com**
    Links to Christian sites

College Press: **www.collegepress.com**
    Christian publisher

Gospel Communications Network: **www.gospelcom.net**
    Huge site of Christian miniatries

Preaching Plus: **www.preachingplus.com**
    Worship, teaching, and planning resources

Standard Publishing: **www.standardpub.com**
    Christian publisher

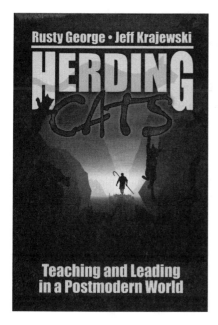

Herding Cats
Teaching and Leading In a Postmodern World
Rusty George, Jeff Krajewski

What could be harder than herding cats? Is it even possible to get such independently minded creatures all heading in the same direction? To church leaders dealing with the postmodern mindset of the so-called Generation X and Generation Y, cats might seem well behaved and highly trainable by comparison. Rusty George and Jeff Krajewski write from experience in suggesting ways to achieve the impossible. Just as cats will do what you want them to if they are sufficiently motivated, there are ways to help postmoderns decide to follow and serve the Lord. Rusty and Jeff tag-team a thorough examination of the problem and suggested solutions, and have also enlisted the help of others in providing case studies in the last two chapters of workable ministries for postmodern "cats."

220 pages, soft, #CL-873-9 $11.99

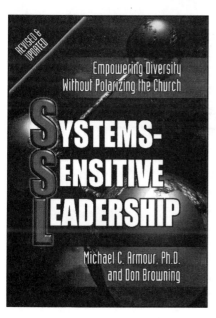

Systems-Sensitive Leadership:
Empowering Diversity without Polarizing the Church
Michael C. Armour and Don Browning

God demonstrated his creativity even in our personalities. People view events from different perspectives and presuppositions. Whether it is conflict resolution, goal achievement, or completing a specific task, a systems-sensitive leader will be able to recognize the differences in people and help them to work together toward common objectives. This is a must read book for anyone involved in church or business leadership.

300 pages, soft, #CL-814-3, $14.99

I'd Rather See a Sermon:
Showing Your Friends the Way to Heaven
Dave Stone

Many people will never hear a sermon. Christians, however, are walking sermons. This great book can help you make a difference in the faith of people God brings you in contact with. You can touch lives with the message of grace and forgiveness. Evangelism doesn't have to be difficult or complicated. In an easy-to-read format, Dave Stone will guide you toward a more effective way to bring your friends to Christ.

154 pages, soft, #CL-865-8, $8.99

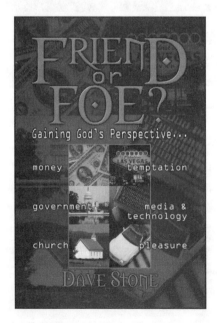

Friend or Foe:
Gaining God's Perspective. . .
Dave Stone

Tackling such issues as money, government, church, temptation, media and technology, and pleasure, Stone helps us to see that we can find God's intention in these tough areas of our lives. If you have struggled to walk faithfully in any of these areas in your life, then you will greatly benefit by reading this book. With his creative, easy-to-read style, Stone will help you understand how your perspective can help you live a life that honors God in the face of challenging issues. Study questions at the end of each chapter make this a great resource for small groups or Bible classes.

128 pages, soft, #CL-867-4, $9.99